You Sound Like a White Girl

The Case for Rejecting Assimilation

Julissa Natzely Arce Raya

FLATIRON BOOKS
NEW YORK

 For information, address Flatiron Books, 120 Broadway, New York, NY 10271.

www.flatironbooks.com

Grateful acknowledgment is made for permission to reproduce from the following:

"Remembering Those Taken from Us" (page 122): *Time* magazine, "It's Long Past Time We Recognized All the Latinos Killed at the Hands of Police" by Julissa Arce © 2020

"In the Name of Whiteness" (page 27): *Time* magazine, "Trump's Anti-Immigrant Rhetoric Was Never About Legality—It Was About Our Brown Skin" by Julissa Arce © 2019

"Mexican American Disambiguation" by José Olivarez (page 139) © 2018

"How English Came to Me" by Janel Pineda (page 70) © 2021

Library of Congress Cataloging-in-Publication Data

Names: Arce, Julissa, author.
Title: You sound like a white girl: the case for rejecting assimilation / Julissa Natzely Arce Raya.
Description: First edition. | New York: Flatiron Books, 2022. | Includes bibliographical references.
Identifiers: LCCN 2021041591 | ISBN 9781250787019 (hardcover) | ISBN 9781250812810 (ebook)
Subjects: LCSH: Assimilation (Sociology)—United States. | Americanization. | Minorities—United States—Social conditions. | United States—Ethnic relations.
Classification: LCC HM843 .A73 2022 | DDC 303.48/2—dc23
LC record available at https://lccn.loc.gov/2021041591

Our books may be purchased in bulk for promotional, educational, or business use. Please contact your local bookseller or the Macmillan Corporate and Premium Sales Department at 1-800-221-7945, extension 5442, or by email at MacmillanSpecialMarkets@macmillan.com.

First Edition: 2022

10 9 8 7 6 5 4 3 2 1

For the people of El Paso, Texas.

For all the Mexicanos who never left.

For the ones that just returned.

For paisanos everywhere.

Contents

Introduction

The Case for Rejecting Assimilation

> *I coveted whiteness once, but I knew in the back of my mind that conning myself into assimilation would only ever make me a poor imitation of what I would never be.*
>
> —Reni Eddo-Lodge, *Why I'm No Longer Talking to White People About Race*

A runner ties her shoelaces and is ready for the race. She's prepared to run the 400-metre dash. As the starting pistol goes off, she's informed that her race is now the 400-metre hurdle. She's stunned but determined. She clears the first hurdle, barely—she has not trained for this race. It slows her down, but she resumes her stride. She struggles to clear the second hurdle. By the time she gets to the next hurdle, she's starting to get the hang of this race she never knew she'd be running. There is a hint of a smile on her face because she's finally catching up. Suddenly, the ground is slick with water beneath her feet. She looks around, but it is only in her lane. How is that possible? She has no time to ponder such mysteries, for the next hurdle is here. She clears it. Gravel is thrown in her lane, and she loses her footing. But she is strong and agile, and with one foot in front of the other she clears the remaining six hurdles. As she's about to run through the finish-line ribbon, she's told that her race isn't over. She must complete another lap around the track, and when she's done, she can claim her spot on the podium. She's exhausted, but she must finish, so off she goes to run her final lap. She finishes in record time. Along the way people cheer and tell her what an amazing job she is doing. As she puts her arms up in celebration, she's once again informed that her race continues. Frustrated and out of breath, she goes around the track once more. She wants desperately to be off the track and on the podium. By the tenth time she's gone around the track, she begins to wonder if someone like her is meant to finish the race. None of the runners who now have medals around their neck look like her. She presses on. After years of running around and around, buying new kicks, getting new coaches, inching closer, she falls chasing a finish line that she was never going to reach. She picks herself up, looks at her bloody knees and hands, and wonders what the hell she is doing.

Finally one day she stops running, walks off the track, and goes in search of something better. Something more truthful. Something closer to freedom.

◦ ◦ ◦

When I was a junior in high school, a boy I had a crush on told me I sounded like a white girl. I had spent so much time practicing how I enunciated words so no one could tell English was my second language that I took it as a compliment, though he had not meant it as one.

I was still undocumented in high school, so sounding like a white girl gave me a false sense of security. Having an accent said I was from someplace else; sounding like a white girl fooled me into thinking I could belong in the United States. If I sounded like I was from here, who would question whether I should actually be here?

I am a Brown, formerly undocumented immigrant from Mexico. Assimilation has been forced upon me since the moment I set foot in San Antonio, Texas, in 1994. For a long time, I didn't understand that assimilating to "American" culture really meant imitating white America—that "sounding like a white girl" was a racist idea meant to tame me, change me, and make me small. I ran the race, completing each stage, but I never quite fit in. No one told me I was entering into a system that never wanted me to begin with.

My parents ate American exceptionalism like it was holy communion on Sunday. They were the first people to fall for the lie. They told me everything was possible in America as long as I worked hard and stayed out of trouble. This idea proved too simplistic, too naive. When

I became undocumented at the age of fourteen, after my tourist visa expired, doors began to close. I thought with my smarts, with my English, with my money, I could blend in and slip through the cracks unnoticed. Once I was in, I'd integrate, I'd latch on, I'd become a part of the United States. I'd belong.

I learned the language, at the expense of my Spanish, only to find that in English I didn't exist. I read the American history textbooks in school that erased any trace of the deep Mexican roots in this country. Still, I forged ahead. I received a college education, graduated with honors, and landed a prestigious job, only to find that it wasn't enough. I needed a piece of paper with a nine-digit Social Security number, something that eluded me.

When you are someone like me, you can't get to the top without bending the rules because the rules are meant to keep you at the bottom. So with fake papers I managed my way to one of the most coveted jobs on Wall Street. At Goldman Sachs I made enough money to be considered upper middle class. I paid taxes, gave back to my community. But despite my superficial success, plenty of people wanted me to go back to where I came from.

I thought, W*hen I get my papers, my parents' formula will work, and everything will be possible, everything will be okay, everything will be beautiful.* I got my green card in 2009. The process nearly cut me in half: the anxiety of each application, every fingerprint, the fact that my entire life depended on an immigration official's mood. My body expressed all the things I didn't have the words to scream. I had unexplainable headaches, searing back pain, and a stomach too weak to belong to a Mexican. I was the oldest twenty-six-year-old in the world.

Two years later, in 2011, I left my corporate job at Goldman Sachs. To my mom, my decision felt reckless, like throwing away the fishing pole that had kept us fed and jumping into the open water. She viewed the security of my paycheck as more than money. Instead, it was a reward for everything we had endured as a family, most of all the pain of being separated from our loved ones in Mexico and eventually from each other.

I had *made it*. I had the career, the money, y papeles. Ya lo tenía todo. Hadn't I reached the finish line of a long race I had been running since the moment I immigrated to the United States? Why walk away after everything I had been through, when I had survived it all and finally had what we immigrated for: a better life, a 401(k), and papers? But how many scars had I collected along the way, many still unhealed, still stinging? My decision was necessary, urgent even. I was a fish needing to get back in the water.

I told my mom how walking away from the security of a paycheck was actually the biggest flex of all. I joked, "Mira ahora me pagan para criticar al país." Who would have imagined: we thought we had to be perfect, and now I make a living pushing this country to do better by us.

In August of 2014, twenty years after I arrived, I became an American citizen. By then the process had exhausted me—the legal dance, for sure, but what had truly gutted me was the undertaking of assimilation. I was asked to do the impossible: to shed my heritage and become white. I wouldn't get to remain who I was, like the snake who sheds its skin to grow and heal after an injury but remains a snake. I had to become someone else, thinking one day the race would be over and I'd finally be able to wear America proudly around my neck. Americanizing was supposed to help me fit in, but even after I learned English, became a citizen, got my coins, I still wasn't welcomed. In fact the opposite was true. To still be Mexican, I had to speak Spanish, a language that escaped my tongue the more time I spent here. Many Mexicans told me I wasn't Mexican enough, though I was born in Mexico and spent the first eleven years of my life there. I was caught in the middle, rejected by my own people while the American identity still dangled out of my reach. I had to put myself back together and almost didn't survive the transformation. I became a Frankenstein collecting the pieces I'd lost along the way—my language, my culture, my family.

I needed to write this book to heal. In researching the stories of our past, I found the truth I had been missing. This book is about dismantling the lie of assimilation to reclaim the most essential and beautiful parts of ourselves, our history, and our culture. In the first half, I will dismantle the lies that drive immigrants, and people of color, to change who we are in order to make us palatable, or at least tolerable, to white America. I didn't find freedom in assimilation because there is no freedom in racist ideas. Assimilation requires that the story we tell about the United States and about white people is an uplifting, inspiring, sugarcoated version of the facts, in which the whip, guns, and racist motives must remain hidden. But it was the truth about this country, the knowledge of its ugly dirty secrets, that set me free. In part one, I talk about the lies. The lie of whiteness that distorts the history of our country to cast white people as the saviors and everyone else as invaders. The lie of English that says if we learn the language and speak it like a white person, we'll be treated with dignity. In reality, English has been used to segregate us in schools, to keep us from voting, to deport us. Then there is the lie of success, which makes us believe that as long as we pull ourselves up by our bootstraps like the good European immigrants of the past, we'll surely earn our place. When some of us do reach positions of power, the assumption many white people make is that we must be the affirmative action student or hire. We end up believing and spreading these three lies, but belonging doesn't exist in racist America, it exists in our America. In the places we build for ourselves.

As much as we talk about America the melting pot, the nation of immigrants (another lie), the beacon of light in the world, the balance of power remains overwhelmingly white. The top ten richest Americans, all white. The U.S. government is 87 percent white in Congress, and 99 percent of governorships are held by white people. The publishing industry, 76 percent white.[1] TV executives who decide what media we consume, 88 percent white.[2] In education, 75 percent of full-time college professors and 80 percent of teachers are white.[3] Yet, so many of us set out to climb the corporate ladder thinking we can be one of those top ten richest Americans without fully understanding the racist policies that will make it nearly impossible. Or, without considering how becoming a billionaire hurts people, our people most of all.

The lies of assimilation culminate in telling immigrants that if we do it "the right way," we'll be welcomed with open arms. But there is only one correct way to exist in America, to have unquestioned belonging, and that is to be white. I will dive into how citizenship laws that go back as far as 1790, when the first U.S. Congress was formed, were created to exclude people based on their color and race. Chinese immigrants were banned from entering the United States after they started to move up the economic ladder. Mexican immigrants were recruited to come work the fields, only to become disposable scapegoats. When economic hardship hit, their families were deported en masse, whether undocumented or U.S.-born. Legality has never protected us.

Assimilation is not a road to belonging, but rather the carrot America dangles in front of immigrants, Latinos, and other people of color, an unreachable goal to keep us fighting for the single place at the podium rather than spending our energy creating spaces where we don't have to compromise who we are to fit in.

With the marked rise of white nationalism in the United States, there is an urgent need to reject the idea that America is a country with a singular identity that only one group of people gets to call home. The demographics of America are changing; some estimates suggest white people will no longer be the majority as early as 2045.[4]

Though it might be tempting to think that with Donald Trump no longer in office, the worst of American racism and hatred is over, we would be wrong to believe that the illness that is racism is behind us. Donald Trump was simply a symptom. During the attempted coup on the U.S. Capitol on January 6, 2021, the Confederate flag was flown inside the building for the first time in history, but the white supremacy it represents has roamed the halls of Congress all along. And it is still there.

We'd also be foolish to believe that only white people are capable of perpetuating white supremacy. We are all caught up in a system designed to help advance white supremacy by replicating the behavior of our oppressor, sometimes out of ignorance, for protection, or because we have a false belief that we, too, can become white, and therefore have the power, money, and privileges white people do.

So how do we untangle ourselves from the web of lies? In the second half of this book, I share how we can fight our way back to true freedom and belonging through reclaiming our history, our identity, and our culture. When I was a young girl learning about the history of the United States, I often asked myself, *Where were we?* I've learned that Mexicans, our Indigenous ancestors, have always had a footprint in this land. We have many examples to follow of people who resisted assimilation, who fought for equality. We must shine a light on those who came before us, those who showed us decades ago that we are enough. Through them, I have learned this is where I belong, not because white people accept me, but because the same roots that ground me to Mexico ground me here, too.

I am a Mexican immigrant, and my experiences as a Brown Latina have informed how I view my place in the world. It's a complicated story. Where do I, as a non-white, non-Black person, fit in binary conversations about race that dictate life in America? And in turn, how does my non-white, non-Black identity contribute to the power of white supremacy?

Reclaiming my identity has been a painful birthing process. Something beautiful has been born, but not without blood and tears. The Latino identity is complex. As I write about in more detail later, even the very words we use to describe our community cause controversy. How we are counted in official forms like the census have created unintended consequences, or maybe it's by design that we are treated as America's bastard child, as perpetual foreigners no matter how many generations ago we became American. At times I argue that Latinos should not aspire to whiteness because it's never offered protection or belonging. That argument becomes complicated because there are Latinos who are white. Unpacking all of this felt like taking a thorn out of my ribs—an experience full of pain and relief at the same time.

Some people say that I am ungrateful because this country has given me so much, and that I should simply ride into the sunset with the bounty it has bestowed upon me. The truth is, I do have a lot, but I finally know how much it has cost me. In order to love America fully, I had to stop being enamored with it. To me, there are two Americas. One doesn't want me now and never will, no matter how many human-interest stories we tell or facts we chart. I am not interested in writing for that America. I used to think we had to preach beyond the choir if we wanted to create a better world. Narrative change strategies have been focused on transforming the way people see us, on convincing white people to view us as human through our stories of pain, success, and trauma. But now I know the choir needs energizing, needs love, needs to feel seen, heard, and understood. I am glad other people are doing the work to change hearts and minds. But my work focuses on changing how we see ourselves. On empowering us, both in our feelings and in our actions. This book is for the choir—a choir of whoever can relate or find meaning in these pages. I welcome you into this space.

I love us. I believe in us. We don't need the kindness of the white gaze to celebrate ourselves. We don't need our stories to be translated so white people can see us as human. They are not our saviors. We are.

It is time to thrive in our own skin. It is time we learn our history and stand in our truth. The future and health of our nation depends on our willingness to embrace, support, love, and celebrate all the people that create the United States. That will happen only when we stop trying to be accepted, when we stop viewing whiteness as the center of the universe, as what we should assimilate to, and when we create our own spaces and make our own antiracist rules.

I am Mexican, and I am proud of it. I am also American, and that's not a separate identity from my Mexican one. I don't live between cultures. I am both cultures. I carry all of it in this gorgeous brown body. No matter how hard this country has tried to get rid of us, we are still here, flourishing. My hope is in us. In me. In you.

PART ONE
The Lies We're Told

· 1 ·

The Lie of Whiteness

The Gringo, locked into the fiction of white superiority, seized complete political power, stripping Indians and Mexicans of their land while their feet were still rooted on it. Con el destierro y el exilio fuimos desuñados, destroncados, destripados—we were jerked out by the roots, truncated, disemboweled, dispossessed, and separated from our identity and our history.

—Gloria Anzaldúa, *Borderlands/La Frontera*

The Baggage That Immigrates with Us

For the first eleven years of my life, the pieces of my cultural identity were not spread across borders. I was a Mexican in Mexico. If I ever felt like I didn't belong at school, it was not because I was ethnically different. The culture was mine. I was Mexican with no quote marks. I didn't need to eat spicy food to prove it. Taco trucks weren't a fad, and I didn't need English-language documentaries to explain what makes a taco a taco de guisado. Eating the food, speaking the language, dancing to the music—it was all like breathing air.

Still, I began to learn the importance of whiteness as a child in Mexico. I was told by my lighter-skinned grandma not to spend too much time in the sun or I would get even more prieta. The only time I was allowed to wear my hair parted down the middle was on El Día de la Virgen de Guadalupe, the one day out of the year when I should look Indigenous on purpose. If my words had grammatical mistakes, my tías would say, "Te pareces a una Chalitla," even though I probably am a Chalitla, like the other Indigenous people in our region of Guerrero. My grandmother heard those same sentiments from her grandmother. In an effort to spare children from the same contemptuous mockery, we tell them to marry someone who is lighter skinned so they can help "improve the race." The casta system set up by the Spanish during colonial times to socially rank people based on their proximity to Spanish blood, with those who were white and born in Spain at the top of the hierarchy, has been officially dead for centuries, but we keep perpetuating it by repeating the message that lighter skin is more valuable to the next generation. When I was a little girl, I wasn't able to discern these racist displays by my family, but I did internalize them.

Whiteness is celebrated in every area of Mexican life, so I aspired to hold the beauty of white Mexicans on my face, on my skin, and in the roots of my hair. The problem wasn't just at home. The media we consumed also shaped how my family and I viewed ourselves and those around us. I saw white Mexicans on TV, in magazine ads, on billboards. White Mexicans sang my favorite songs from Luis Miguel's "Cuando Calienta el Sol" to Paulina Rubio's "Mío." Thalía starred in my favorite telenovela, *Marimar*. If darker-skinned Mexicans appeared in telenovelas, they were portrayed as the help or the evil mistress, or they were caricatures of Indigenous or Black Mexican culture. It wasn't until July 2020 that the first Indigenous Mexican model, Karen Vega, who is Oaxacan, graced the pages of *Vogue México*.

In 2019, when Yalitza Aparicio was nominated for an Oscar for Best Actress for her lead role as Cleo in the film *Roma*, Mexican racism tore through the thin linen shade where it pretends to hide. Famous telenovela star Sergio Goyri was caught in a viral video, calling Aparicio "una pinche india," who didn't deserve her nomination. The only one who did, according to Goyri, was Alfonso Cuarón, the film's white Mexican director. Further, to help make Yalitza more palatable to a Mexican audience, magazines like *¡HOLA!* photoshopped her to look lighter, skinnier, and less Indigenous. Many Mexicans deny the possibility of any of us being racist because, as Goyri said when confronted by the press, "a proud Mexican cannot be racist." But so many of us are still covered in the ashes of colonization.

When I was about eight, I was playing in El Zócalo with some friends from school when an Indigenous girl approached us to sell candy. One of the light-skinned girls started taunting her, saying she smelled like caca. Another girl said, "Qué fea prieta, déjanos en paz." I looked very much like that Indigenous girl, except I was wearing a Catholic school uniform. I joined in on the ridicule, telling the Indigenous girl, "Ni siquiera hablas bien español!" I hoped that in my insults the other girls didn't recognize the indigena in me. I resemble mi abuelita Enedina, my dad's mom, who was Indigenous. But we didn't talk about that at home. Instead, my mom would tell us how mi abuelo Pedro, who died when my dad was seven or eight years old, looked like a Spaniard. She would say, "Qué bueno que tu papá no se parece tanto a su mamá," Except he did. My dad had beautiful dark skin, and thick hair and full eyebrows. When I was a newborn, my mom buzzed my entire head to get rid of my curls, because they reminded her of my abuelita's.

I sometimes think about the girl in El Zócalo and ask her for forgiveness.

One of the hypocrisies in Mexico is that we learn to be proud of the mighty Aztecs who built the pyramids, but not of the Indigenous person who has survived all these centuries, who speaks Nahuatl or one of the other sixty-eight Indigenous languages still spoken in Mexico.[1] Mexican pesos are decorated with the Aztec calendar. We take school trips to Teotihuacán, to experience the glory of our Indigenous past, but we don't pay any attention to the present-day Indigenous communities in desperate need of resources. We can take pride in the heritage left to us by our Indigenous ancestors and at the same time reject that we are in fact still Indigenous, too.

The song of our colonizers plays the moment we are born despite more than two hundred years of Mexican independence. If you spend enough time around your Mexican family, you've undoubtedly heard someone brag about their "abuelito de ojos azules." We want so badly to be white that some of us will claim our mother's grandpa was from Spain, even if he wasn't. Even if by doing so, we are belittling ourselves.

For Black Mexicans, the erasure and racism are even more prevalent. Mexico has hidden an important part of our history. After the Spanish were done killing Indigenous peoples and still needed to enslave people for profit, they brought Africans to the American continent, whom they viewed as "strong for work, the opposite of natives."[2] As Ibram X. Kendi points out in *How to Be an Antiracist*, Indigenous people were viewed as weak, and that justified our genocide just as the perceived physical strength of Black people justified their enslavement. A few Africans also arrived as free men and were conquistadores.

Black Mexicans have been part of our story for centuries. Yet they have had to fight to be recognized as Mexican. The year 2020 marked the first time the country counted Afro-Mexicans as part of the official census. In 2015, Mexico's statistic institute estimated the Black

Mexican population to be around 1.3 million[3], yet their history remains obscured and whitewashed.

My nephew, a junior in high school in Mexico, was visiting me in Los Angeles a couple of years ago when I asked him if he knew that Vicente Guerrero, the second president of Mexico, was Black. "Are you serious?" he said. "In all the pictures he looks 'bien blanquito.'" Because of his stature, he could not be ignored or erased from history, but his standing didn't stop him from being whitewashed. Even when negating the history and importance of Indigenous and Black people simply can't be done, we are not allowed to claim power alongside our Indigenous or Black identities—the identity must then be erased. This strategy is deployed from Mexico to the Dominican Republic to Europe.

Vicente Guerrero was the son of a Black father and an Indigenous mother. Inspired by the Haitian Revolution, Guerrero fought to end African slavery in Mexico some thirty years before it was abolished in the United States. Schools all over Mexico bear his name. It's tragic to think that our people in Mexico died to gain independence, freedom, and equality for the Indigenous worker and for the enslaved African, but many haven't been able to shake the colonizer in our heads. A document of twenty-three principles for the future of a free Mexico, called the *Sentimientos de la Nación* written by José María Morelos Pérez y Pavón in 1813, included the prohibition of slavery "forever," as well as the abandoning of the caste system, and only "vice and virtue" making people different from one another. When John Quincy Adams was secretary of state, he wrote a letter to his brother in 1818 in which he described America's independence as "a War of freemen, for political Independence," and Mexico's as "a War of Slaves against their masters." Adams was right that Mexico's independence—as well as the independence of other Latin American and Caribbean countries—was different. The independence of the United States was one where elites sought liberty only for themselves and for the protection of their land and property, which included African people. Mexicans won our independence from Spain to free the most oppressed, even if it hasn't played out that way.

We've been so beaten down by white supremacy that we have yet to be truly free. Whiteness infiltrates Mexican institutions and life just as it does those of its neighbor to the north. It is a problem that plagues much of Latin America. In Bolivia, for example, the first and only Indigenous president came to power in 2006, 181 years after the county's independence. Colombians have taken to the streets to protest racist police, because Black people are killed more often there, too. From Brazil to Mexico, Indigenous and Black people remain oppressed.

When I go back to Mexico now, I am deeply saddened to hear the same everyday racist talk I heard when I was as a kid. I often wonder if I had stayed in Mexico, would I see clearly how we've been tricked to yearn for whiteness so that we don't strive for justice?

I often think of a brilliant line by author Domingo Martinez when I grapple with our own people becoming the oppressor when they've known the scourge of whiteness: "There is nothing more potentially hostile than the indigenous ego interpreting the laws of his conqueror upon his own people." We become vicious to our own bodies, to our own souls. In our own home countries we learn to view white as superior, as something we should aspire to. Then when we immigrate to the United States, we bring those sentiments packed in our suitcases. Those ideas are hardened on our hearts like a wax seal the minute we cross into the United States.

Mexico introduced me to the lies of whiteness, but it was the United States that taught me just how corrosive white supremacy truly is. Seeking whiteness is a matter of survival here: white skin in the United States means you exist. It means you matter. Some of us flatter ourselves white by virtue of our education, our job, or our bank account—despite the nopal on our faces, we introduce ourselves as "Spanish" at work. In the United States, whiteness didn't just render me less than—it rendered me invisible. Here a Brown Mexican seems to have no past, no future, and no identity. I was further ostracized because I was undocumented. It was the ultimate layer of being alien. But here, in my new home, is also where I learned to fight it.

When White Became White

A few years ago, I was at a birthday party, talking with a friend, when a white woman introduced herself. As is natural in this kind of setting, she proceeded to ask us how we knew the birthday girl. "We went to college together," I responded.

She then asked where we were from, to which my friend Kevin replied, "I'm from Brownsville." Not satisfied with his response, she asked where his parents were from. Once more he said, "Brownsville." This is a scene I've watched before. I squeezed the drink in my hand so hard I thought I might break the glass. She continued her interrogation with a question every Latino has heard: "But, I mean, where are you *from* from?" The answer was once again Brownsville. She snapped and hissed, frustrated that Kevin wasn't giving her the response she was fishing for. To her, and to many people, all Latinos are immigrants, presumed to have arrived with wet backs across the Rio Grande.

I jumped in and asked her where *she* was from. She said she was from Jersey, her parents were from Jersey, and before Jersey, "Well, I am just white. My ancestors are all American."

American equals white equals American. Were her ancestors Italian, Irish, German, Dutch, Ukrainian? Historically, not all Europeans were welcomed with open arms, but how quickly white Americans take refuge in their whiteness. Immigrants from Southern and Eastern Europe were not considered white enough when they first immigrated across the Atlantic. Their arrival felt like a corruption of American life and a downgrade in the genetic makeup of the country—they were viewed as illiterate and too docile.[4]

A white person today can simply say, "I am white; therefore I am American," but a Mexican with centuries of history in this land must explain where we are *really* from.

How is it that European immigrants become unquestionably American? How did white skin became the determining factor for claiming Americanness? It was not a matter of language acquisition, or success, or patriotism, as some claim. Germans, who in the nineteenth century constituted the largest non-English-speaking immigrant population in the United States, continued to speak their native language exclusively, and often their U.S.-born children didn't speak English, either. Even fifty years after arriving in the United States, many of them spoke only German.[5] European immigrants were not smarter or more hardworking. They did not become American by virtue of their success. The tenements in the Lower East Side of New York City demonstrate that European immigrants came largely from the working class, impoverished people scrapping by to survive. Still, by the twentieth century, Greek, German, French, and other European immigrants sat comfortably under the umbrella of whiteness, as decisively American.

Instead, becoming white has long meant standing on someone else's neck. It's also been about bargaining away your culture and vying for a better position in humanity's made-up hierarchy. The poet Diane di Prima speaks to how this was true for early European immigrants: "[Whiteness] was not something that just fell on us out of the blue, but something that many Italian Americans grabbed at with both hands . . . they thought, as my parents probably did, that they could keep these good Italian things in private and become 'white' in public."[6] In other words, becoming white meant trading in Italian culture, language, food. It meant assimilating. In *How the Irish Became White*, Noel Ignatiev explains that the Irish not only had to leave their roots behind but had to define themselves as different and above Black people. Back in Ireland, many were against slavery, but upon arriving on the shores of the United States, they were willing to part with their beliefs if it meant holding on to the privileges of whiteness in America. They opposed emancipation, fearing that Black people, no longer enslaved, would flood the labor market and they'd be left on the street. How American to place the value of a job above that of Black lives. Frederick Douglass liked to point out that his old job at the plantation remained open should any white man like to apply.[7]

As white immigrants were brought into the fold, my people were further excluded. The whiter others became, the more non-American we became. The Mexican-American

War, in which the United States illegally invaded Mexico, served to solidify the notion of Europeans as patriotic Americans and Mexicans as trespassers. Nearly half of the U.S. soldiers in the war were foreign-born, but they became lauded as patriots. "The Killers," as the most savage battalion was called, were hailed as heroes for their display of the "extremest of bravery." By executing Mexicans, European immigrants earned their Americanness—their whiteness. They were too willing to accept that Mexicans were like dogs with no breed, a lesser race, and they were therefore justified in taking Mexican land, in killing us.*

Many historians have studied the complexities of how European immigrants became American, but it's hard to ignore what they all had in common that other groups of immigrants did not—their white skin. European immigrants assimilated and gained power because whiteness was available to them. That's what made them American. That's what made grandiose myths. This country many times uses them as a shiny example of what immigrants should be, as a backdrop of everything we are not. But white became white by excluding others.

Today, there is no hope of becoming American in the way America demands—the white way—for those who come from a "shithole" country, as Trump famously labeled

---

* To be fair, there was also a group of mostly Irish immigrants who deserted the American army and fought on the Mexican side, forming the Saint Patrick's Battalion.

places like Haiti, El Salvador, Nigeria, and other countries in Africa. "[N]ow that our immigrants are overwhelmingly poor Brown people, the rules of political correctness require that we submit to their culture," writes Ann Coulter, an extremist who has played a major role in crafting the national conversation about immigrants in conservative circles. She maintains without irony, "we no longer ask anything of immigrants in terms of assimilation. We can't. That would be 'racist.'"[8] But the opposite is true. We demand assimilation, knowing that no amount of it can offer belonging because our brown skin can never be made white.

In the Name of ~~Patriotism~~ Whiteness

One summer day I visited a friend in a suburb of Dallas, Texas, and I got lost in the winding dead-end streets. It was bright daylight, but I was scared. I was an undocumented Mexican, driving without a license, since Texas denies them to undocumented people. Every single house, replicas of one another, had a U.S. flag hanging from their white porch. I still hope one day the American flag will be a welcoming sign of unity that I can fly from my home without inadvertently sending a message that people like me don't belong. But these symbols today feel like a scar from a toxic relationship I took too long to leave. The battle wounds of assimilation still sting in my body. The wind that day was hardly blowing, and instead of dancing on the breeze, the red and white stripes sagged, looking sad, as if bogged down by all the racist ideas embodied in it. By all the horrors Americans have committed in the name of freedom, for the sake of patriotism.

More than a decade later, a twenty-one-year-old white man walked out of a house just like the ones on that street and drove for ten hours, from Allen, Texas, just outside of Dallas, to El Paso, as he later confessed. I wonder if he saluted a U.S. flag before he walked into the Texas heat. He must have chosen El Paso with its large Mexican American population on which to inflict the most pain. He must have chosen a Walmart on a week when back-to-school shopping was at its highest to protect *his* country from Mexicans, from people who look like me, as though America was not also ours.

On August 3, 2019, he took his AK-47 and targeted and killed twenty-three mostly Latino men, women, and children. His goal was to kill "as many Mexicans as possible" and to stop the "Hispanic invasion of Texas," he wrote prior to the shooting in a manifesto authorities believe he authored.[9] He didn't just mean people of Mexican heritage or undocumented Mexican immigrants, but Brown people who he understood as Latino (given police officials say he fired indiscriminately). He didn't stop to ask any of the twenty-three people he killed for their papers, or if they came to the United States "the right way" or immigrated "legally." That's because it wasn't about legality. It wasn't about assimilation. It was a racist act. It was about our brown skin in America. It's always been about that.

It was only a matter of time before dangerous words became dangerous actions. Peter Brimelow, an extremist who, according to the Southern Poverty Law Center, "warns against the polluting of America by non-whites, Catholics, and Spanish-speaking immigrants," writes in *Alien Nation*: "The American nation has always had a specific ethnic core. And that core has been white."[10] If by white he means exclusionary and racist, then I agree. *Alien Nation* was published in 1995, but the narrative of Latinos as outside the American core, as foreigners, as threats, has been at the center of American history, past and present. America has denied that our people have always been part of this land. "We are a nation besieged by peoples 'of color' trying to immigrate to our shores," writes another right-wing extremist, David Horowitz. As long as Latinos continue to be viewed as invaders, we are in danger.

In September 2019, Trump asked during a rally in New Mexico, "Who do you like more—the country or the Hispanics?" The framing of this question separates Latinos from America. It ignores the fact that in the United States, Americans and Latinos are one and the same. There are more than 60 million of us, and 80 percent of Latinos under thirty-five are American-born.[11] In Texas, 70 percent of Latinos were born right here in the USA. *The Guardian* found Donald Trump used the word *invasion* when referring to the southern border and the need to build a wall in more than 2,000 Facebook ads in a nine-month period.[12] *USA Today*, in a study of five dozen rallies and events, found that Trump used words like *invasion*, *criminal*, *predator*, *killer*, *animal*, and *alien* more than five hundred times when speaking of immigrants.[13] Nativists have used the idea of Latinos "taking over" as a means to get rid of us, discreetly through racist policies and violently with AK-47s.

It is not just members of right-wing fringe groups that espouse the view that Latinos are foreigners. In *Politico Magazine,* Adrian Carrasquillo reported on the hurt, fear, and pain Latinos experienced in the aftermath of the 2019 shooting, even in the "liberal" city of Los Angeles. He wrote a story of his friend's husband who "overheard white men at the community pool remarking that while they didn't agree with the killings . . . they, too, didn't want white people to be 'wiped out' and for Hispanics to 'take over.'"[14] How novel of them to stand against the murder of Latinos. This rhetoric perpetuates the idea of Latinos as foreigners no matter their immigration status. That we *are* American didn't matter to the shooter in El Paso or to the very people who we've hired to represent us. Texas Senator John Cornyn dismissed the terrorist act as a "very complex problem," to which "sadly . . . like homelessness . . . we simply don't have all the answers."

This reluctance to call the massacre what it was—a

terrorist act carried out by a white supremacist against Latinos—is just as damaging as loading a gun. Not everyone needs an AK-47 to hunt Brown bodies to be complicit in our deaths. But these white men will continue to wear a U.S. flag pin on their fancy suit jackets and demand that we love their country, the same country that has tried time and time again to "send us back to where we came from." They will hide their rotten souls behind patriotism, with flags flying from their porches.

These nativists—these racists—imagine a U.S. utopia of white people that has never existed. We've been here. Mexicans, and more broadly Latinos, have never invaded Texas. Our land was stolen, and now we're the ones who are viewed as thieves. White supremacy doesn't care if we are here legally, or if we were born here, or if our families have roots in America dating back centuries, perhaps even longer than theirs. The fear many white people have is not whether we will assimilate, but whether our Latino bodies, and those of our children, will roam this land.

August 3, 2019, will forever be marked in my heart. I wailed in pain that day. For those who were viciously killed in cold blood. For those of us left behind who were filled with fear and worry for ourselves and our children. The crushing weight of assimilation was also lifted off my shoulders that day. I saw it so clearly. So many of us have tried to learn English, to get a good job, to become citizens. But even when we do, we still have to watch our backs at Walmart.

When Mexicans Became "White"-ish

The first colonizers to arrive in what is now the United States were not the pilgrims in 1620. It was the Spanish, who came to New Mexico in 1598. The oldest capital in the country, Santa Fe, New Mexico, was founded in 1610 by Don Pedro de Peralta, a Spaniard who was born in Mexico. This is not a point of pride but a part of our complicated story. The Spanish colonizers in search of riches were not the only ones to arrive in northern Mexico. Along with priests looking for souls to save, many Indigenous people came—some as servants, others forcibly to quench the lust of men, some as wives, and many more for endless other reasons.

After gaining its independence from Spain, Mexican authorities attempted to increase the population in its northern territory—a land that stretched all the way up the west coast of California and across to the Rocky Mountains—and so welcomed Anglo immigrants. By 1834, more than 30,000 of them lived in Texas, heavily outnumbering the Indigenous, mestizo, and Black Mexican population, along with Spanish people born in Mexico, of 7,800.[15]

Mexico abolished African slavery in 1829, decades before the U.S. Emancipation Proclamation in 1863, but those Anglo immigrants had brought with them more than 5,000 enslaved people in violation of Mexican law. This is where the story needs some revision. Texas's independence from Mexico and eventual annexation into the United States is often told as a freedom fight. But let's be clear, Anglo Texans wanted to be "free" in order to keep Black people enslaved. They became legends while stealing Black bodies, stealing Mexican land, and terrorizing native Tejanos.

The Mexicans who stayed in Texas were treated as second-class citizens in the Republic of Texas, an attitude that still pollinates along with the bluebonnets, their stories lost to white historians. As scholar Neil Foley stressed in *The White Scourge*, "In Texas, unlike other parts of the South, whiteness meant not only not black, but also not Mexican." The horrors that Mexicans suffered in Texas at the hands of Anglos have been buried in forgotten graves, in cemeteries that no longer exist. However, in Texas history classes, Davy Crockett, William B. Travis, and Jim Bowie die heroes at the Alamo, killed by the vicious Mexican army. This is of course a fairy tale, still retold in museums and textbooks. They were visitors, undocumented immigrants even, and by proclaiming self-rule, they forced Mexico into war.

Many of us understand that America was built on the brutality of slavery and the looting of Indigenous land. Fewer recognize the colonization of Mexico by the United States as a third pillar in the creation of present-day America. The first colonization of Mexico was of course by Spain. But the second colonization of my people came at the hands of the United States during the Mexican-American War. In school we learn of it as Manifest Destiny, as the God-given right of white people to steal native land. The result was not only the taking of land—present-day New Mexico, Utah, Nevada, Arizona, California, Texas, and Western Colorado—but the reluctant acquisition of Mexicans.

Less than ten years after becoming its own nation—which was never recognized by Mexico—Texas was annexed by the United States as the twenty-eighth state of the union at the end of 1845. The annexation of Texas into the United States and a dispute over where the Texas border should be drawn gave President James Polk an excuse to loot more Mexican land while expanding the pro-slavery territory. There were between 80,000 and 100,000 Mexicans living in the land stolen by the United States. Polk wanted the land, but not the Mexicans on it. They were never immigrants; they didn't come to the United States or cross the border; the border crossed them. After the war, the Mexico-U.S. border was carefully drawn to keep as many Mexicans out as possible, a purpose it still serves. But the border never stopped our roots from growing on both sides.

As a compromise of war, the United States begrudgingly guaranteed American citizenship for these Mexicans when the Treaty of Guadalupe Hidalgo was signed by both countries in 1848 to end the war.* As a result, Mexicans threw a wrench in the racial dynamics of America, and in turn, our place in the United States has been precarious ever since, because we became citizens at a time when only white people could become citizens, even though most of us were not white. In 1790, the very first Congress of the United States had established by law that "free white persons," of "good character," who had resided in the United States for at least two years were the only people eligible for naturalization. Not even Native Americans, whose land was stolen, whose women were raped, and who were killed in a genocide, were accepted as U.S. citizens until 1924.

The United States wasn't happy about giving citizenship to Mexicans. After all, Mexicans were viewed as racially inferior, primitive creatures who were ignorant and knew nothing of laws.[16] *New York Times* articles from the 1870s and 1880s note how the "Lazy Mexicans" were "retarding progress." We were described as "the personification of tramphood" on the front page of the *Times*. Another racist piece stated, "Greasers as citizens. What Sort of State New-Mexico Would Make." Our "origin and character," our "hatred of Americans," and our "dense ignorance" made us "totally unfit for American citizenship."[17] We

---

* Whether Mexicans became U.S. citizens immediately has been disputed by historians. Some sources say it took years for them to be recognized as citizens. Others say some Mexicans never became citizens at all, because they were never able to claim it.

were an undesirable compromise for manifesting a white destiny in the West.

What became of those first Mexicans in the United States, an unwanted bounty of war, has had a lasting impact on the visibility of our struggles in America. By granting those Mexicans citizenship, the United States effectively made them *legally* white, but our rights as Mexicans were never codified in the law. There were no amendments to the Constitution. Nothing explicitly said that, as Mexicans, we had protections, that we were equal. American citizenship for those Mexicans was a Trojan horse, a loophole of whiteness, leaving it to the courts to decide when our legal whiteness gave us rights or when it was used as an excuse to take them away.

America has always viewed us as a problem—what to do with us, where to place us, where to discard us. America has also fooled us into thinking that we can attain whiteness, and that when we do, it will cover us and keep us safe. It does not.

Just as the Mexico-U.S. border was drawn to include the smallest number of Mexicans possible, so were new territories accepted as states based on how many Mexicans were present. Texas was annexed as a state because the white immigrants outnumbered the Mexican and native population.[18] California became a state two years after the end of the war because of the gold it held, the value of the precious metal rendering the presence of Mexicans easier to accept. But the rest of the territory, including New Mexico—which at the time constituted the majority of the stolen land, where Mexicans and Pueblo Indians made up most of the population—did not become a state until sixty-five years later. For more than six decades, Mexicans in that area could not vote or run for office. Arizona was also left behind, and in 1909, the territory enacted a law that made speaking English a prerequisite for voting and running for office. The Arizona Rangers were then created for the purpose of enforcing this new law, with state-sanctioned violence against Mexicans.[19] Perhaps this was an attempt to prove how loyal to white America people from Arizona could be. Three years later, Arizona was finally annexed as a state.

Mexicans weren't the only Latinos who were not wanted. Puerto Rico was not seen as a place where the majority population would ever be white, and therefore it was not fit for statehood. To this day, Puerto Rico remains a colony of the United States. Puerto Ricans, while U.S. citizens, cannot vote in presidential elections and have no voting representation in Congress.

In New Mexico, white liberals and the Mexican elites found a path to gain statehood in assimilation. A white man named LeBaron Bradford Prince, the "grandfather" of New Mexico statehood, embarked on a whitening effort to lead the territory into the union. He did it all wrong. His fight wasn't to gain equal rights for Mexicans as Mexicans, but instead for us to be accepted as white. He, like many today, tried to claim and glorify Mexicans' Spanish blood. Mexican elites, many of whom were visibly lighter skinned than Indigenous Mexicans, were more than happy to run with this idea. In fact, they actively sought to distance themselves from Indigenous and Black people, as they had done during colonial times. But the majority of the citizens of New Mexico were Pueblo Indians and Mexicans of mixed Indigenous, African, and European blood. It's debatable if Prince's strategy worked, or if New Mexico was finally accepted as a state in 1912 because enough white people had moved there.

In stealing our land, in making us legally white, the United States took so much more than it gave with citizenship. It reiterated the message of our first colonizers, that our Indigenous and African ancestry were to be disregarded and hidden. It pushed the early Mexicans of the United States to distance themselves from their true roots in order to lessen the blow of the white hand. It killed our ability to seek civil rights. How could we claim to be oppressed if we were (legally) white? It may have felt necessary at the time to claim whiteness, but what did it accomplish? What did we gain from the scraps given to us by white people? We were in a no-man's-land. We didn't receive the rights of white people, only the illusion.

"The Right Way"

The problem, as I've heard on cable news, in conservative circles, in entertainment media, was not that I was a Mexican immigrant, but that I was "illegal." Had I come over legally, my presence in this country would not offend. Never mind that for most undocumented immigrants there is no application they can fill out or process they can go through, not even a fine they can pay to start the process of becoming U.S. citizens—that's what immigration reform would allow them to do. But if we just did it the "right way," if we just got in the mythical "line," America would welcome us with open arms—so they say.

Sometimes it's other Latinos who utter this nonsense. It's infuriating when Marco Rubio or Ted Cruz, two Cuban Americans, talk about their families immigrating to the United States "the right way." Cubans were embraced as political refugees after the Cuban Revolution in 1959. The "legal way" for Cubans then, and for many decades after, was to arrive in the United States. Their journeys were dangerous ones, but once they got here, they automatically received work authorization, legal status, and access to welfare, health benefits, and more. They could get papers with their wet back. Many of the early Cuban immigrants were among the island's wealthiest and most educated families—people with the resources to pick up and leave. Ironically, as Professor Laura E. Gómez points out, "some of the Latino immigrants [like Cubans] with the most human capital in terms of education and job skills have . . . received the greatest assistance from the federal government in becoming established in their new nation."[20]

People often ask me why I didn't fix my immigration status after my visa expired. The short answer is the immigration laws of this country. I would have to go back to Mexico to get a new visa, which was almost impossible. I had lived in the United States on a tourist visa that allowed me only to visit. My parents' financial situation had drastically changed, and to get a visa, one must not be poor. Applying for a renewal could mean being ripped from my parents. It was a risk we weren't willing to take.

Given the current immigration laws, signed by President Bill Clinton, when someone lives undocumented in the country for more than a year, and they leave the United States, they cannot come back for a minimum of ten years, if ever. I consulted a lawyer every year, but for more than a decade their answer was always the same: until the law changes, there was nothing I could do. It didn't matter if I spoke English, if I had a college education, if I had landed a prestigious job. None of it mattered. Papers do not define undocumented people, but the lack of them certainly outlines much of our lives—what we can and cannot do, what we do anyway. I didn't remain undocumented because I wanted to—no one does. It's better to have papers than to not have them. Living without authorization leaves you fearful every other day, and yet, somehow, we don't break.

I was still an undocumented immigrant when I landed my job at Goldman Sachs in 2005. I was hiding in plain sight because most people imagine that undocumented immigrants stay in the fields, breaking our backs. I wish there had been a legal option to obtain work authorization, but there wasn't. No path to citizenship existed, then or now, for undocumented people. So I did the only thing I could do to keep on: I bought my papers from a woman in Texas. For a few hundred dollars, she sold me a fake Social Security number and a fake green card.

That day I became a criminal in the eyes of so many. Y de ahí no me suben ni me bajan. I used to be ashamed of having broken the law. But not anymore. I now recognize how the law was breaking me every single day.

It was ironic, really, that the only reason I became eligible to adjust my status was because I married a U.S. citizen. I laugh when I think about the many times my mom told me, "You have to be independent. Make your own money. Don't depend on a man." I did, I made my own money, but I still needed a man to save me from my illegality.

After I got married in 2008, my lawyer was able to submit my application to become a permanent resident. The initial retainer was $5,000. I think about how few people have that kind of money. The process put so much stress on my young marriage. The romance was overrun by documents, interviews, and appointments with lawyers and the government. Still, I was one of the lucky ones, because in March of 2009, I received my green card.

I was able to remain in the United States while my application was processed because my initial entry into the country had been with a valid visa. Had I crossed the border illegally, it might not have mattered that I was married to a U.S. citizen. People who had to cross faced the possibility of having to leave the country to process their applications. But as soon as they do, they are hit with the ten-year ban I was afraid of when my visa expired. It's unfair that I became a citizen on August 8, 2014, while many people remain undocumented because they don't have the resources, the luxury of entering the country with a visa.

Even now, as a naturalized American citizen, strangers write to me saying I should go back to Mexico. "You are not a legitimate American," one person wrote. Another was more creative, calling me a "trifling illegal immigrant." The email continued: "You are a disgrace. A fraud. You should NOT be in this country." When I naturalized, I believed that my U.S. passport finally proved I belong here. I thought that all the fears I had while living undocumented would be erased: fears of being separated from my family, of being detained, of being deported, of never being fully accepted in this country. Is naturalizing after years of living in the United States not enough? What does make a "legitimate American" citizen? My critics argue that I became a citizen only because I married a citizen, and I agree that shouldn't be the only way. They say I broke the law, but the law says I could adjust my immigration status only after I married. They will continue to make excuses because they cannot say what they really mean: that they don't want this Brown Mexican body in America.

Since the moment the first Mexicans became part of the country, the United States has tried to send us back to where we came from—without understanding that where we came from is the very land they stole from our ancestors. Mexicans have been here for centuries, since before it was called the United States, and throughout that confusing, painful, and untold history, our U.S. citizenship has been up for debate, our Americanness a question mark, because race, more than any other factor, has driven immigration and naturalization law.

The exclusion of people of color is not limited to immigrants. Those born on American soil to undocumented parents are often termed "anchor babies," their mothers accused of having crossed the river for the sole purpose of giving birth here, their child's citizenship up for debate. In 1898, the Supreme Court ruled in *U.S. vs. Wong Kim Ark* that native-born children of immigrants, even those barred by racial exclusionary laws, were still birthright citizens. A judge proclaimed that "birthright citizenship is protected no less for children of undocumented persons than for descendants of *Mayflower* passengers."[21] If nativists want birthright citizenship to go away, they would need to change the U.S. Constitution, which is why, in 1995, Elton Gallegly, a GOP congressman, suggested such a move, again revealing the racist attitudes toward Brown immigrants. But if we are anchor babies, it is only because we have been connected to this land for generations.

Papers do not produce acceptance. Who is called an American, who deserves to be here, who is worthy of citizenship goes beyond legality and paperwork. This has never been about papers, but about how this country is wrapped in its racist ideas and racist policies.

In 1896, Ricardo Rodriguez, a Mexican citizen, sought to naturalize after ten years of living in the United States. He'd been part of the large number of Mexicans who moved to Texas to fill labor shortages created by the exclusion of Chinese workers in 1882. Anglos, who'd been successful in preventing the naturalization, and therefore voting power, of other groups of people, tried to do the same with Mexicans.

Anglo businessmen looked at Rodriguez's case as an opportunity to settle that Mexicans were not white, and therefore not worthy of citizenship. We may have forgotten we weren't white, but white people never do. The Treaty of Guadalupe Hidalgo said nothing about future Mexicans wanting to become citizens. It was again up to a white judge to find us worthy.

His case could've been used to set a precedent for

future naturalization cases for Mexicans. It could have been groundbreaking by giving Mexicans rights written into the law. Instead, Rodriguez's lawyers won his case by claiming Ricardo was white, even as he was characterized as "having dark skin and Indian features."[22] And alas, we continued to be reminded of our fragile standing in our own land.

In 1945, Private Felix Longoria was killed in the Philippines while serving in World War II. Upon the return of his body, in 1949, his family wanted to make use of the local chapel in Three Rivers, Texas. The director of the funeral home refused because Longoria wasn't "white." A Purple Heart veteran, a fallen hero, who lost his life serving his country, was denied burial because "the whites would not like it." His citizenship rights did not protect him against whiteness, not even in death. Had his family been allowed to use the chapel, he would still have been buried on the Mexican side of the cemetery.

Longoria was not the only Mexican, or Latino, veteran to face discrimination after the war. Dr. Hector P. Garcia, a war veteran, founded the American G.I. Forum precisely because Mexicans faced systematic racism, even those who served the country. Garcia was deeply involved in getting justice for Longoria's family. As national attention built, radio commentator Walter Winchell called out the entire state, saying, "The big state of Texas looks mighty small tonight." Lyndon B. Johnson, a senator at the time, got involved and helped to arrange burial for Private Longoria at Arlington National Cemetery. Under immense public pressure, the Texas House of Representatives conducted an investigation into what became known as the Felix Longoria Affair. Not surprisingly, the committee found that no discrimination had taken place by the funeral director.

In 1952, Congress finally did away with race, sex, or marital status requirements for citizenship. Race requirements for naturalization are now considered illegal, but I'd argue that the lack of immigration reform over the past thirty years is equivalent to a racial bar for Latinos and other immigrants of color, who remain undocumented without a path to citizenship. All this time later, we are still fighting for our right to be called Americans, to receive equal rights.

In 2013, under the guise of protecting the security of state birth records, Texas denied birth certificates to children of undocumented parents. Without birth certificates, these U.S.-born mostly Latino children struggled to access basic services like education and health care. The state settled a lawsuit and has resumed making these important documents accessible, but such behavior continues across the country. During the administrations of George W. Bush and Barack Obama, and into the Trump era, the State Department denied passports to people who were delivered by midwives, as opposed to in hospitals, along the Mexico-U.S. border in Texas. Midwife births are a long-standing tradition in Mexican culture, but officials accused these citizens of using fraudulent birth certificates procured by the midwives. They say these Latinos were actually born in Mexico. Natural births outside hospitals are now trendy among wealthy white women. But their babies aren't detained in immigration detention centers, nor do these women's children face deportation after applying for a U.S. passport with legitimate U.S. birth certificates. No, that only happens when you are born with brown skin.

In July 2019, Francisco Erwin Galicia, a Dallas-born teenager, was held in Immigration and Customs Enforcement (ICE) custody for nearly four weeks, where he says he lost 26 pounds due to the poor conditions and was not allowed to shower. In March of 2019, Customs and Border Protection detained nine-year-old Julia Isabel Amparo Medina, a U.S. citizen, for more than thirty hours when she crossed the border at the San Ysidro port of entry to attend school.[23] These are not isolated incidents. ICE requested the detention of 3,076 American citizens from October 2002 to December 2018, according to Syracuse University's Transactional Records Access Clearinghouse.

In the United States, it is not enough to be born on American soil or to naturalize or to live out your days here. It is not even enough to serve in the nation's military. In 2019, the U.S. Government Accountability Office released a report detailing how over the past six years hundreds of veterans have been placed in deportation proceedings.[24] The total number of deported veterans is unknown. This lack of information is purposeful. If we don't know the severity of the problem, it loses urgency. Our right to be here has been up for debate over centuries of civil right fights, changes in the laws, and public discussion.

Let's free ourselves of the notion that there is a right way to become American. Let's rid ourselves of the idea that proximity to whiteness will make us American. We've flirted with whiteness, but it's never loved us back. Our youth experience higher rates of depression than their white peers because of this endless race for belonging.[25] We are getting sick, because we internalize the idea that assimilation will make us part of America. But no matter what we do, we are still stereotyped as lazy criminals who bring drugs and who rape white women. We are treated as foreign invaders who must be met with handcuffs and bullets. It does not matter how many Mexicans or Latinos there are in the United States, our place in America will never be secure if we keep seeking acceptance on the basis of whiteness.

Pretending to be something we are not will only give us a feeling of constant alienation. If we can feel strong, smart, and accepted only because the white gaze looks at us with kindness, then what are we, really? If we're ever to receive full rights, we must do so on the grounds that as Brown people, we deserve them. Because we do.

In 2018, I had the privilege of welcoming new American citizens at their naturalization ceremony in our nation's capital. It was surreal, to have been undocumented and now to stand in front of mostly Black and Brown immigrants and to welcome them to America—to tell them that in their Brown bodies, in their Black bodies, they deserve to be here.

· 2 ·

The Lie of English

English . . . was the language of money, domination. Six-foot Mexicans would wither when its sounds were spoken by a five-foot-tall white man, make them hunch their shoulders, lower their heads, and move in the direction opposite the English . . . English was power.

—Domingo Martinez, *The Boy Kings of Texas*

English Doesn't Make Us American

My parents spent nearly two decades in the United States before returning to Mexico. They never became fluent in English. My mom could hold whatever conversations she needed to have, using her hands, trying again and again until she was understood. She hasn't lived in the United States in almost twenty years, but she still remembers some English. She is so proud of the words she knows, as though in English her words are worth more. My dad was a fast learner, but though he understood English well, the use of one wrong word could make him forget everything. English drained his confidence.

Once when I was a child, we went to a Taco Cabana

where pretty much everyone spoke Spanish. He began placing his order in Spanish, as he had many times before. But this time, English greeted him. He tried to explain that he wanted his order in two separate bags, and the woman kept saying, "What? What are you saying?" With each *what*, my dad's English became more infused with fear. I still have a feeling the cashier spoke enough Spanish to take my dad's order, but she wanted to feel tall by pretending she didn't understand him.

I didn't speak English then, so I couldn't step between my father and racism. A Latina behind us helped him place our order. I saw the embarrassment in my dad's body: his eyes lowered; he shrank down. Each time something like this happened to him, he retreated further and further away from English.

I've seen this so many times. How in English we become more afraid instead of more confident—how often it robs us of our dignity. "I was scared that I could not speak English, and that in turn made me scared I could not do the job," Julián, who is a day laborer, told Karla Cornejo Villavicencio in her book *The Undocumented Americans*. And yet, Karla writes, "I think every immigrant in this country knows that you can eat English and digest it so well that you will shit it out, and to some people, you will still not Speak English."[1]

Like many Latino immigrants in the 1990s, my parents bought *Ingles sin Barreras* after seeing a million advertisements for it on *Sábado Gigante*. The set contained various

VHS videos, cassette tapes, workbooks, a dictionary, and a pronunciation course. Their ads didn't just sell the ability to speak another language—they sold a better life. If only you spent the time and money, you'd achieve all your wildest immigrant dreams. But the reality was different.

My parents spent more money than they could afford to purchase the program. Then they had to pay off the debt by working more, leaving them with less time to open the books. Where does one find the time to learn English when there are children to feed? When family in Mexico is depending on our remittances? Even with time and money, people find it challenging to learn another language, especially as adults. It is no wonder that, according to the U.S. Census Bureau, only 20 percent of Americans can have a conversation in two or more languages. Spanish doesn't make us less than, it makes us uniquely skilled.

My parents viewed learning English as a matter of survival. They didn't need anyone to demand that they teach their children. They saw it as a first step to finding success in America. When I immigrated, I spoke only Spanish. My mom enrolled me at a Catholic school where English as a Second Language (ESL) classes were not available. As a child, I found it traumatizing to be thrown into an environment where I could not communicate, express my thoughts, or push back when ridicule came my way. While I learned English, I was able to take open book tests, which I still often failed. My classmates and even my own teachers saw the extra help I received as indicating I had learning difficulties. I felt a drive to prove them wrong.

My parents constantly reminded me that I wasn't here "para jugar a las comiditas." They had brought me to America to be successful—to make good on their sacrifices. Learning English was important to improve my grades, to help my parents with their business, and eventually to get a good job—to achieve the American dream. But English is the first lie of assimilation.

My mom hired a private tutor to teach me English after school and on the weekends. I knew the financial sacrifices my parents had to make to afford private lessons—making sure it was all worth it fueled my tongue. Every day after school I spent hours studying my flash cards to expand my vocabulary with new words and idioms. The summer before seventh grade, I attended an expensive summer course that solidified my proficiency.

As soon as I could speak, write, and read in English, I became my parents' primary translator. I translated bank statements, letters from the principal, unpleasant negotiations with the landlord, and even heart-wrenching conversations with doctors when my mom had a nearly fatal accident. But because I was a child speaking to adults on behalf of adults, I never knew if any of those people took me seriously, or if they laughed in words I couldn't understand.

By the time I graduated from middle school, I was fluent. I even had dreams and thoughts in English, which made me feel like I was betraying my parents, the entire country of Mexico, and my dead ancestors. My tongue moved in ways that weren't in my DNA. Still, I took such satisfaction when my teachers would say, "You speak English so well now, you can barely notice your accent." As a child, I didn't realize how patronizing those comments were. What saddens me even more now is remembering the pride my parents felt when one of their friends would comment how "pretty" my English was because I sounded like the gringos.

But my accent still showed up to terrify me when I wasn't paying attention. I had not yet learned to love the texture of my English. From time to time my *three*s came out as *tree*s. One day in eighth grade, we were reading about animals, and the word *crocodile* appeared in the text. I pronounced it as *cocodrile*, resembling the Spanish word cocodrilo. My classmates roared with laughter. It didn't matter that I was an honor roll student: one bad move and I was back to being the dumb Mexican girl who couldn't speak English. It was exhausting having to be perfect or unearth the ugliness in people.

Yes, learning English propelled me forward. But no matter how much I studied, my English continued to fall short. Sounding like a gringa didn't make me American, and it didn't give me the privileges of one. The bone-crushing realization that even with English we aren't enough gives survival a bitter taste.

It's not just the words, but everything they project: confidence, entitlement, and power.

Watching LaKeith Stanfield play Cassius Green in the film *Sorry to Bother You* reminded me of all the times I've had to sound like a white girl to be taken seriously. Stanfield plays a telemarketer having a hard time making sales. Boots Riley, the film's director, describes Cassius using his white voice to land a sale as discovering "a magical power" which "disguises the fact that he is actually Black." Hearing him describe it as "magical" punched me in the gut.

When I let go of my white girl voice, I was reminded by my Wall Street bosses that certain colloquialisms, a word I still have a hard time pronouncing, were not professional. I was dumbfounded to learn that screaming "Fuck!" while pounding the desk was acceptable behavior, but saying "yo" was not. I have a joyful laugh that fills any room. The volume of my voice offended just as much as my manner of speech. After my boss told me I was too loud, I learned to tame my laughter. This was a reminder that taking up space will make others uncomfortable because they only want to see us quiet and thankful.

The first time one of my Goldman Sachs clients asked me to bring him coffee because he mistook me for the assistant, I was embarrassed for him. I felt like I was the one who had to make up for his racism, the burden falling on me to make him comfortable. And isn't that twisted? I told myself he had made an honest mistake since I looked so young. The truth was much uglier: having a Mexican woman advise him on how to protect and grow his precious money was not something that this white billionaire was used to.

After that occasion, I never went to a client meeting unless I had spoken to them on the phone first—using my white girl voice, of course. Assimilation forces us to erase, or at least hide, who we really are by dangling an illusion of success in front of our faces. I figured that if they could first hear my ideas, then they would know I was a smart and capable investment professional. But even if they didn't ask me to serve them food and drinks, there were other subtle ways they reminded me that my white voice didn't fool them. Comments that I was "so well spoken" and my speech so "eloquent" served as reminders that, in their mind, someone like me wasn't supposed to have a mastery of words.

English, no matter how many of its words I mastered or how much of its magical power I harnessed, did not protect me from the powerful race dynamics that labeled me foreign. A white voice did not make me American. My English still trembled with a desire for acceptance.

Assimilation, whether linguistic, cultural, aesthetic, or otherwise, always has more steps to complete. As you master one, more appear. I honed my speech to sound like the popular white girls in my school, like the blond all-American girls I saw in movies and on TV shows. I stood in front of a mirror, saw my brown reflection, and tried to imagine the girl speaking back to me was someone white, someone whose words brought her pride and confidence. I cry when I think of that Julissa. I want to hold her and tell her one day she'll laugh when she texts her friends, "I am going star crazy," and they write back, "Comadre, qué es star crazy? Like stir crazy but more galactic?" She'll respond, "We can all be star crazy with a little herb from the earth," and roll on the floor laughing so hard her tummy will hurt.

My husband pokes fun at me whenever I make use of the wrong idiom or use the incorrect word in a sentence. He finds it endearing. My friend Carlos has a running list of all the things I say wrong, and we joke about it over drinks in a pool in Palm Springs. In my accent, in my mistaken words, in my imperfect English, I've found laughter and joy.

English Segregation

In the seventh grade, I was placed in an honors math class. I barely spoke English at the time, but math is a universal language. When the names of the students who were placed in the honors class were read and mine came up, a boy interrupted.

"Why is *she* in the honors class?" he said. "She's *a Mexican*! She doesn't even speak English!" It's a lie that all youth will lead us into a better world. Some will repeat the same hateful behavior they learned from their parents, who learned it from their grandparents.

That was more than twenty-five years ago, but it was not the first or last time a Latino child was met with disdain in the language that is supposed to give us belonging. More than giving us a national identity, English is a violent river that drowns us. That boy had wanted to keep me separate on the basis that I didn't speak English, a strategy used by school districts all across America to enforce school segregation between white people and Mexicans.

While this fact is not broadly known or recognized, school segregation for Latino children was common in Texas and California, where 80 percent of districts in 1931 were officially segregated and the other 20 percent had off-the-record segregation rules. In 1930, the elementary school in Lemon Grove, near San Diego, California, built a barnlike structure for 75 Latino students (out of a class of 169). They claimed that the children lacked English skills and that separating them was necessary for the "Americanization" of "backward and deficient" pupils. The Mexican students, school officials argued, could benefit from added attention. Why not send the Latino students to the main building and the white kids to the barn, then, if we needed special attention?

The Lemon Grove Case (*Roberto Alvarez v. the Board of Trustees of the Lemon Grove School District*), or the Lemon Grove Incident, as it was widely called, is the first known successful school desegregation case in America in any court. Many of us have never heard of this case, and sadly we are in danger of losing the evidence forever. The records of the historic ruling have not been digitized and exist only in outdated paper files. The case was won because the court found that Mexicans could not be segregated from the white students because they were "white" themselves and ordered the school to integrate.

Two earlier lawsuits, one in Tempe, Arizona, in 1925, and one in Del Rio, Texas, in 1930, had tried to make the same argument: Mexicans couldn't be segregated because we were legally white, and if we were white, we weren't different. Except we were. These cases backfired, ironically for the same reason the other case was won. The courts in Arizona and Texas determined that since the plaintiffs were "white," they had no grounds to argue that they were racially segregated. Despite the school superintendent commenting that "some Mexicans are very bright, but you can't compare their brightest with the average white children. They are an inferior race," no basis for discrimination was found, and the schools remained segregated.[2]

The ramifications of the Treaty of Guadalupe Hidalgo are in full display in these cases, despite their different outcomes. That pesky "legally" white label kept delaying true justice for my people. Our rights as Mexicans were never codified in the law, and so it remained that our supposed "whiteness" was the determining factor for our fate. We kept having to fight the same battles over and over. Sixteen years after the court ruling in Lemon Grove, another Latino family had to struggle for their daughter to attend an integrated school. In the 1940s, school districts across California set up "Mexican" schools because officials argued that Mexicans could not keep up with "Anglo-American" students, again using English as the excuse. In 1944, Gonzalo and Felicitas Mendez tried enrolling their children at their local school in Westminster in Orange County, California, and were turned away. Mr. Mendez insisted that his children, who were Mexican and Puerto Rican, and all other Latino students should be given an equal education. When the school district refused, he joined four other plaintiffs and sued.

In 1946, the district court found that the assignment of students was at times purely based on the students' Spanish last name rather than on their English skills. *Mendez v. Westminster* marked the first time school segregation was legally struck down in federal court for Latino students. The district appealed, but the case was once again won in the 9th Circuit Court of Appeals in 1947. While there were no official laws that mandated segregation of Latinos, as there were in the South for Black students, the court ruled "the equal protection of the law" applied in this case "because the practice of segregating Latinos in public schools violated the state and federal constitutions." The school districts were ordered to integrate Latino students.

Before *Mendez*, there were laws that segregated Asian and Native American children in the state, and as a result of the case, Governor Earl Warren outlawed the racist policies. Seven years later Warren became the Chief Justice of the Supreme Court when it presided over *Brown v. Board of Education*, the landmark case that legally ended school segregation for African American students. The Mexican struggle was not cited in *Brown*, though, because Mexicans are not considered a racial group. The NAACP did file an amicus brief in the Mendez case, and later called the case "a trial run for *Brown v. Board*." But for sixteen years, courts did not interpret Brown as prohibiting the segregation of Latino students.[3]

As school districts began to intergrate, bilingual education programs were squashed as backlash. English, always on its toes, finds new ways to separate us. In 1998, California voters passed Proposition 227 by a wide margin, eliminating bilingual educational programs. The law required students to be taught in English only. Latino students suffered greatly as a result. In 1998, the high school dropout rate for Latinos was 37 percent.* After a significant push from Latino activist groups and other social justice organizations, Proposition 227 was replaced in 2016 by Proposition 58, which allows schools to decide how best to teach their students, bringing back bilingual programs. By 2019, the dropout rate had fallen to 7.7 percent.[4] White supremacy is persistent, but so are we.

Today, according to U.S. Census data studied by *Child Trends*, one in four children under the age of eighteen is Hispanic/Latino.[5] Nearly 3.8 million English learners are native Spanish speakers who are not proficient in English.[6] Only 67 percent of students without English proficiency graduate from high school in four years (compared to 84 percent of all students). Children will learn when they are given the resources, but American cities and states refuse to support and serve the needs of their students. Arizona, where Latinos make up 45 percent of the student population, still upholds a law that forbids English learners from receiving instruction in their native language and requires the separation of Spanish-speaking students from their peers. Sooner or later, we will have to realize that the future of the United States rests on the well-being and success of all Latino children, including those who do not speak English.

---

* In 1998, 7.7 percent of white students ages sixteen to twenty-four dropped out of high school, compared to 14 percent of African Americans and 37 percent of Latinos. By 2019, the dropout rate for Latinos decreased to 7.7 percent, and to 6.5 percent for African Americans.

How English Is Used Against Us

One night at dinner, I lamented to a couple of friends. "We are asked to talk, walk, dress, be like Americans. But it doesn't matter if we learn perfect English. It's never enough."

"But if you don't learn English, then what holds us together as a nation?" one replied.

My friend's statement stung a little—or a lot. Was English all that was holding us together? And if so, why were the resources needed to learn it withheld? Why was belonging never a side effect of speaking it?

I paused before responding. "I think most immigrants *want* to learn English. But we should learn because it is good for us, because it makes our lives easier. Not because white supremacy demands that we do." The demand is always cloaked in racism. It's never issued out of compassion or an offer of help. The underlying message is always *If you don't speak English, you don't belong here.*

Perhaps if English met us where we are, instead of making us feel small, instead of making it difficult to hold our head up high, we might learn it without resentment, without scars. But that is not how the demand to assimilate works. Assimilation puts the burden of success or failure on us, the immigrant, the person of color, the Latino. Almost every English learner I have ever met has a story of how English crushed them at a young age.

My friend, the award-winning author Reyna Grande, wrote that on her first day of school in the United States, her teacher sent her to the "farthest corner of her classroom," where she was ignored for the rest of her fifth-grade year because she didn't "speak a word of English." She writes: "I was made to feel shame, when instead of a door being opened, an invisible wall was erected, when instead of being celebrated, my mother tongue was degraded."[7] If Spanish is ever completely lost in the United States, it will be the result of hundreds of years of discrimination. In another instance, a mentee of mine told me that in elementary school she was placed in special education classes because her teacher took her silence in English as an inability to speak at all. She was in the wrong classroom for a week, but it was long enough to carve into her heart that if you don't speak English, your voice doesn't matter.

In February of 2019, Sergio Budar was speaking Spanish to two employees at a Mexican restaurant in West Virginia when an older white woman named Jill exploded with anger. "Get the fuck out of my country," she said to Sergio in a viral video.[8]

He tried to explain *in English* that he is a U.S. citizen and that the problem is not his Spanish but the views she espouses. The woman continued to berate him: "I don't have any problem with the way you look . . . You are in America, you need to speak English."

The entire conversation took place in English, so Sergio patiently asked, "What do you think I am doing [if not speaking English]?"

Finally, another customer, a white man, stepped in and called the woman a racist, to which she responded, "I am not a racist!"

Even as she retreated from the restaurant, she continued her attack. "I got raped by illegal aliens, but I am supposed to be nice to you? You can't speak English . . . Rapists!"

I will always believe women, and a rape accusation should never be taken lightly. But to justify her need for English to be spoken in her presence, she conflated not speaking English with being undocumented—with being a rapist.

It is not against the law to speak Spanish. In fact, it is not the law to speak English, as the United States does not have an official language. Thirty-two states have gone through great lengths to institute laws, or change their state constitutions, to make English their official language. Montana is one of those states. There, immigration enforcement operates as though it is a crime to speak any other language. In May 2018, Ana Suda and Martha Hernandez were shopping for milk and eggs at a convenience store in Havre, Montana, when they were stopped by U.S. Border Patrol.[9] The small town is about thirty miles south of the U.S.-Canada border and home to a CBP (Customs and Border Protection) field office. When Suda asked the CPB officer on cell-phone video why they were asked for their IDs, he responded, looking directly into the camera, "Ma'am, the reason I asked you for your ID is I came in here and I saw you guys are speaking Spanish, which is very unheard-of up here."

The ACLU filed a racial discrimination lawsuit pointing out that the border patrol agent, Paul O'Neill, commented on the women's "very strong" accent, and asked them where they were born. Ms. Hernandez and Ms. Suda were born in California and Texas, respectively.

After presenting their Montana driver's licenses, Ms. Suda and Ms. Hernandez were able to go on their way. But if they had been undocumented, they would've been taken into custody and potentially deported. Ms. Suda can be heard in the video saying, "I am a U.S. citizen and I have my rights." But sadly, when you are a Brown person speaking Spanish, you don't.

As painful as it is, this type of traumatic episode tears us away from Spanish. In a statement to *The New York Times*, Ms. Suda said her daughter only responds to her in English now, "because she is scared [to speak Spanish]." Who can judge her for abandoning the language?

English as a justification for enacting violence has a track record. In 1975, a group of ten Mexican American women, known as the Madrigal 10, filed a lawsuit claiming that they had been sterilized without consent. The judge ruled in favor of the U.S.C.-Los Angeles County Medical Center, saying that it was a case of a "breakdown in communications."[10] They were sterilized like stray cats and dogs, but he blamed their lack of English as the reason why some of them were tricked into signing documents they didn't understand. He went on to say that he believed Mexican women draw their worth from "rearing" a large family, so their pain came not from being sterilized against their will, but because they could not fulfill their Mexican duties.[11] One eugenicist in the 1920s said we were "irresponsible breeders who [flood] over the border in 'hordes' and undeservingly [sap] fiscal resources."[12] Mexican women's bodies were stripped of all humanity; they were seen as "peons" who "multiply like rabbits."[13] So what better way to stop our "breeding" than to sterilize our bodies and blame it on our inability to speak English.

The problem has never been the language, but the people who speak it. While Latinos walk around with a scarlet letter for speaking Spanish, white people are embraced as cultured when they learn our language. Bilingual programs are trending with affluent families. Many schools in America now teach English as a Second Language and well-off parents pay tens of thousands of dollars for dual-language immersion programs, but speaking Spanish while Brown still isn't safe in many parts of America.

A few years ago, I was at a coffee shop in Los Angeles sipping on an almond milk latte, scrolling through Twitter, when a group of white girls sat next to me. They were talking about their study abroad trip to Spain that summer.

One of them said how important it was "in today's market" to speak Spanish. I put my headphones on and kept reading the news stories on my feed. I came across the story of Natalia Meneses and her three-year-old-daughter, who were harassed by another shopper at Walmart for speaking Spanish. The little girl saw some flower hair clips and said, "Mira, Mami!" This was a private moment between daughter and mother. An older white woman who overheard the conversation turned to Meneses and said, "You need to teach this kid to speak English, because this is America and kids need to learn English. If not, you need to get out of this country."[14] Only when *we* have the audacity to use our mother tongue do racists worry about the future of the country, but for others it's an added skill to speak Spanish. For us it threatens our livelihoods, our families, our lives.

I thought about how some white women have taken it even further by cosplaying as Latina. In recent years, there was Jessica Krug, "Jess La Bombalera," a white Jewish woman from Kansas who described herself as Puerto Rican. She is a historian of Africa and the African diaspora. She took on an accent, put on some hoop earrings, and proceeded to publish academic works as a "supposed Black woman."

Then there was Natasha Lycia Ora Bannan, a prominent human rights attorney, who pretended for years to be Colombian and Puerto Rican when in reality she is a white woman from Georgia. In one interview, she says she's a "bridge" for her Latino clients, acknowledging the lack of Latina representation in the legal profession. She was celebrated as the National Lawyers Guild first "Latina" president.

And look, she did it with an accent—accents that create barriers for all of us Latinas in professional settings. "If you really have an accent, you will have very negative experiences in [the legal profession] . . . Several people asked me if I took the bar exam in Spanish. At the time, it was extremely hurtful because I knew they were making assumptions about my capabilities," Ana Gabriela Urizar, a Latina from Guatemala, who practices corporate immigration law, told *Prism*.[15]

When I hear "This is America, speak English," I hear white people's fear that the United States they have known will disappear and be replaced with one where they do not have all the power. One in which they do not get to dictate how others should live their lives.

We are made to believe that English is our savior, that if only we can read the words, we'll be whole. We're told that language is the conduit to acceptance in this country, as if words spoken and written the right way will cloak us with freedom. The truth is that these patriots who demand we speak English with insults, racism, and violence use it as the excuse to make a distinction between them and us. They further draw a line between Americans and supposed non-Americans where the sides are dictated only by the color of our skin. They hide their disdain with an insistence that it is our language that doesn't make us worthy. "If you love America, you must speak English," they say.

But tell me, how are we supposed to fall in love with a country that demonizes us in its language? That calls us illegals, aliens, animals?

English Takes and Takes

now I'm afraid
'cause I bet
English is sitting
somewhere in this room
clutching its stomach

rolling over in laughter
at how I typed these words
sometimes first in Spanish
then backspaced my return to English.

—JANEL PINEDA, *"How English Came to Me"*

I listened to Nestor Gomez tell a story on NPR's *Moth Radio Hour* as I drove down one of those famous palm-lined L.A. streets on a clear Sunday afternoon. He was born in Guatemala and immigrated to the United States in the 1980s. His story was titled "Movie Night,"[16] and I listened closely, rolling up my windows, because each of his words told me about my life.

Nestor spoke about how his brother memorized the capitals of each U.S. state for an oral quiz at school. As he delivered the correct answer with the wrong pronunciation, his teacher and classmates laughed at him. The teacher reprimanded him for not studying. Determined to speak English, Nestor and his brother switched from watching Spanish-language TV to English shows. "We watched Roseanne before we learned that she actually hates undocumented immigrants," he said.

Soon, both brothers became fluent enough to laugh at the English jokes on screen. One movie night, Nestor rented an Eddie Murphy film instead of their regular Mexican movies to watch with their mom on her day off. Their mother sat on the couch watching the movie with them, but she was unable to share in the joy. "[Mom] looked at us with a strange look on her face. She was looking at us like she didn't know who we were. Like we were alien to her, like we were strangers," Nestor said on the program.

I cried listening to Nestor explain how English had created a separation between him and his mom. English is important to navigate life in the United States, but English also cuts the umbilical cord to our mother tongue, to our mothers.

Once English dominated my tongue and thoughts, my younger brother and I no longer spoke Spanish to each other. The closer I was to English, the greater the distance between my parents and me. Perfecting my English didn't just kill traces of my native tongue, it fractured lines of communication with my family. My brother and I loved going to the movies, but my parents didn't often watch with us. Going to the theater is expensive, but more than that, they couldn't understand the films we loved. I wished to be like one of those families we saw sharing popcorn.

When I was eighteen, my parents moved back to Mexico and I was left behind with my English. I never forgot Spanish and still consider myself fluent. But my life in America kept changing while my Spanish vocabulary was stuck in my fifth-grade Mexican classroom. It took enormous effort to pick up the phone and call my mom and dad. I wish I had known from the beginning that learning English was for me, not for other people. Had I known, I would have valued and respected my Spanish more. When I spoke to my parents, my tongue became a Fruit Roll-Up that wouldn't unwind. Physical distance separated us, but my inability to explain the college classes I was taking, the internships I was applying to, or the plans I had for my future—one that they had sacrificed so much for—created a canyon between us. It is one of the most painful aspects of assimilation: the loss of our heritage, language, and family.

Speaking Spanish is a form of resistance, one we've fought tooth and nail for. In November of 1968, Mexican American students in Edcouch, Texas, led walkouts to challenge rules that prohibited the use of Spanish on school grounds. It was the same year that CBS News reported from the Texas Rio Grande Valley that Mexican Americans outnumbered Anglos, and that the Anglos used domination to maintain control despite being outnumbered. One student told Ed Rabel, "[Spanish] is our mother tongue. I don't see why it should be taken away from us." School officials denied that Spanish was banned from school grounds, though they added that they "strongly encouraged pupils to speak English." According to students, that persuasion came in the form of physical punishment. Another student added, "We are born of Mexican American parents and we have to speak Spanish to them. They want us to forget our native tongue. I don't think that's fair for us."[17] Despite this fight, many Latinos have lost the language for fear of continued oppression. One of my best friends, who grew up in the Texas Rio Grande Valley, told me his parents purposely didn't teach him Spanish because they didn't want him to face the same discrimination they faced for speaking it and for the accent it left behind.

At the same time, not speaking Spanish leaves us feeling as inauthentic, incomplete replicas of the Mexicanos, Dominicanos, and Hondureños we are. But Spanish cannot be the only vehicle to claim our Latinidad. I find it both humorous and infuriating when someone tells me they are more Mexican than I am because they eat spicier food or know more Spanish. I was born in Mexico. I am Mexican by birth, by DNA, by heart.

Americanization is a double-edged sword for Latinos in this country. Julián Castro, the only Latino candidate in the 2019 Democratic primary and former secretary of Housing and Urban Development, was asked in an NBC News interview, "You didn't grow up knowing Spanish. Why did that happen in your life?" As I watched, I screamed at the TV, *Why don't you know the history that would help you avoid such a stupid question!* She continued, "For people who don't understand why someone of Latino heritage might not [speak Spanish]?"

Secretary Castro responded, "In my grandparents' time . . . Spanish was looked down upon. You were punished in school if you spoke Spanish. You were not allowed to speak it. People, I think, internalized this oppression." The punishment, the belittlement, the casting of us as aliens and foreigners led many Latinos to want to protect their children by keeping them as far away from Spanish as possible. Castro is a third-generation American. His grandmother came from Mexico in 1922, almost a hundred years ago. How often do we ask white people why they don't speak the language their grandparents spoke, when that language is Polish or Italian or French? As if it wasn't debilitating enough to fend off racists who fault, insult, and detain us for not speaking English, we also have to justify why we don't speak Spanish. Giancarlo Sopo, a

Cuban American media strategist, took to Twitter to share his opinion on why Secretary Castro didn't learn Spanish: "Castro skipped Spanish because he didn't care to learn it, not because he was 'oppressed.'" A comment that is ignorant of the history that scared our Spanish away.

Why don't you speak English? Why don't you speak Spanish? Being Latino in America means the answer to both of these questions holds us to an impossible standard to prove we're both sufficiently American and authentically Latino. I am tired of the interrogation, the unattainableness, the in-betweenness. I am enough to stand on both sides, fully and completely.

In 2019, I attended the Feria Internacional del Libro in Mexico City, one of the most important book festivals in Latin America. It was the debut of *Entre las Sombras del Sueño Americano*, the Spanish version of my first book, *My (Underground) American Dream*. I was full of emotion, fulfilling a lifelong dream to present my book in the country of my birth, surrounded by my family. This was the first time my mom attended one of my book events, since she is unable to travel to the United States. I felt like Frida Kahlo when she finally had a show in Mexico.

I could not have imagined the reception—thousands of people showed up. The front row was filled with my family, who traveled three hours to join me. I was nervous, worried that my Spanish might betray me, that it might quiver with "the sound of aren't you a Mexican?"

as the poet Manuel Paul López wrote. I chose to be open with the audience and tell them that if I stumbled, I hoped they'd extend me grace.

I shared my story with them—how I left Mexico at a young age. How much I missed it all those years I could not go back. How happy I was to be on that stage. The more I spoke, the more my words flowed with power and ferocity, with smoothness and strength. For the rest of my life, I will never forget that October day.

At the end of the Q&A, a man asked a question I cannot remember, but what I will never forget was him saying, "Eres nuestra," and I am Mexico's. La manera que me recibieron jamás se me va a olvidar.

I signed books for a good long while. One of the last ones I signed was for a woman who wanted to correct several of the incorrect words I used in Spanish. But this time I didn't take it. I didn't say thanks for the suggestion. I just told her what I now tell people in English: "I am doing my best."

· 3 ·

The Lie of Success

> *Your Daddy thinks if he works a bit harder, wears better clothes, lives in a nicer home, and buys expensive stuff, white people will respect him. But he's Indian. We're Indian. And Indians aren't white.*
>
> —Charlene Willing McManis with Traci Sorell, *Indian No More*

Not of Their World

Wall Street was a world so different from the one I grew up in. My annual salary as a first-year analyst was $55,000. That's a lot of money, but not as much money as I needed to play the part, to live in New York City and take care of my parents who were back in Mexico. At work I was eating at Michelin-starred restaurants, boarding yachts (financed by a corporate credit card), and shaking hands with millionaires, while at home I was scraping to get by. My roommate and I lived in a one-bedroom apartment with a home office that doubled as my bedroom. We'd shared a Sbarro's pizza special of two cheese slices and a Coke for dinner to make ends meet. But I knew the importance of fitting in. Success on Wall Street didn't just come from hard work.

That first summer I was at Goldman, my boss took a few of us out on the Hudson, in New York Harbor, for a sunset sail. Having never been on a sailboat, I got seasick and spent most of the afternoon trying to keep my food down and drinking ginger ale. Maybe it was a good thing I was in the bathroom most of the time, since I wouldn't have been able to join in the conversations about spring sails to the Bahamas or in my colleagues' complaints that sailing wasn't an official college sport.

When winter came and everyone talked about their holiday plans in Colorado and Utah, I shared with colleagues that I had never been skiing. "How's that possible?" they asked. They could not fathom that I hadn't grown up going to Aspen for Christmas vacation. Many of them still had their parents' credit cards or were living rent-free in spare Manhattan apartments. I wasn't about to tell them that as a child, I was lucky to go to Corpus Christi, a Texas town on the Gulf of Mexico, and stay at a Motel 6. When my family could splurge, staying at La Quinta Inn was, like, wow!

When I told my mom about the new world I was living in—the fancy parties, the trading floor, the business trips that included stays at five-star hotels—she'd say, "It's like the times we took you to Corpus Christi, remember?" I didn't want to get caught up in the shallow Wall Street rut of money and more money, but I desperately wanted to blend in.

One Saturday morning I hopped on a bus to a ski resort in the Catskill Mountains of upstate New York. After a lesson and a lot of falls, I finally got the hang of it. As I made my way down my first real slope, I thought of the rocky state of Guerrero, Mexico, where I grew up. My hometown of Taxco was built on a mountain and was surrounded by lush green hills on every side. But as I looked out from this mountain in upstate New York, it hit me that I had never seen one covered in snow, and here were dozens of them all around me. The sun made the snow shine like glitter. But even as I marveled at the beauty of the whiteness around me, I knew I was not part of it.

The higher I went, the more beautiful the views were. For a moment, surrounded by the beauty of nature, I thought I might belong. Then the Monday after my trip, a colleague asked me about my weekend. Proud that I had finally gone skiing, I told her about my Hunter Mountain excursion. "Didn't you think it sucked? The only real skiing happens out west or in Canada," she said.

My tongue had mastered the difference between *three* and *tree*. My childhood bedroom became a trophy case for my honor roll ribbons, track, basketball, and cheerleading medals. I had made it all the way to the peak of American high society, and still it wasn't enough.

I wish I had realized sooner that no matter how hard I worked, how much success I achieved, or how many dollars I amassed in my bank account, belonging in a white world was not a dividend that came along with it. I had the same job as my white colleagues in the room, but I was mistaken for the assistant. I shopped at the same high-end stores, but I encountered a racist store clerk who took a necklace out of my hands and asked, "Do you know what Prada is?" I ate at the same fancy restaurants, but I was asked by a group of white people to bring them water on my way back to my table after using the ladies' room.

The finish line kept moving. Each time I thought I had done what I needed to become one of them, I was reminded that dressing the part wasn't enough. And thank God for that, because if I'd become one of them, I wouldn't have broken free. Eventually, I left Wall Street. I went back to the mountains, this time with twenty Latino friends. We were loud and it was glorious.

More Than Dollars and Cents

I often think of one day when my dad and I jumped on my bed when I was younger, throwing dollar bills that smelled like grease in the air. It was one of the most joyful moments of my life. We laughed. We declared we were rich! The money we had earned selling funnel cakes during a New Year's Eve festival would be gone in bill payments faster than it took us to make it, but it was the happiest I had seen my dad in many years.

The ability to make payments on time was reason

enough for my dad to be happy, but there was something else driving his joy. Money made being in America worth it—if we were at least better off than we were in Mexico, then all my parents sacrificed to be here would have meaning. My parents never let me forget that grounding myself in financial security was the ultimate goal. They taught me the importance and power of money from an early age. Whenever we were behind on payments, my parents would argue about why they came to America. "¿Para qué? ¡Si seguimos todos jodidos!" my dad would yell. My mom, always a believer in the American Dream, would respond that we might be struggling, but at least in the United States there was always the opportunity to do better. "Si le echamos más ganás, sí vamos a salir adelante," she'd say. There was something true in my mother's statement—as Latino immigrants we did have to work harder and faster to get places. But the problem has always been that once we get to that place, there is more to be done—it never ends. We must prove ourselves worthy all over again.

Wealthy Americans, politicians, and the media have been incredibly successful at painting immigrants and people of color as lazy and happy to live off government assistance. Presidents from Bill Clinton to Donald Trump have excused their anti-immigrant policies by invoking the lie of immigrants as a load that could break the financial system in half. It was Clinton who said, during the 1995 State of the Union Address, "the public services [illegal aliens] use impose burdens on our taxpayers . . . that's why our administration [is] barring welfare benefits to illegal aliens." Trump could've finished Clinton's sentence in a 2018 speech when he falsely claimed: "illegal immigration . . . places enormous strains on local schools, hospitals, and communities in general, taking precious resources away from the poorest Americans who need them most."

Ideas of economic value are heavily, if not entirely, dependent on race and skin color. Of all the pictures in newsmagazine stories about poverty in 1967, a whopping 72 percent were of Black people.[1] At a campaign rally in 1976, Ronald Reagan capitalized on these images, introducing the "welfare queen" as a Black woman. And all these years later, it has stuck, despite all the data showing that white people are the largest recipients of welfare. According to a 2015 Department of Agriculture report, 40 percent of SNAP (food stamps) recipients are white, 25.7 percent Black, and 10.3 percent Hispanic. What is often ignored is that before the 1970s, when 80 percent of immigrants were white, no restrictions existed to access welfare programs like Medicare or Medicaid.[2] It was only when we became browner and more Latino that the country needed to curtail access to these safety net programs. But white immigrants' stories are weaponized against immigrants of color to shame us for needing any kind of government assistance, instead of examining the racist policies that keep us impoverished.

Today the media continues to paint immigrants of color as leeches sucking resources out of the United States, all while accusing us of stealing American jobs. How can we be both lazy low-skilled people and job-snatching thieves? I want to say to them, "We aren't stealing *your* jobs while sitting on our couches eating Hot Cheetos." We leave our families, land, customs, and good food behind to work hard and *earn* a better life in this country. If we were looking to just get by, why risk our very lives? Immigrants don't dream that small. It is a symptom of the system of inequality that some immigrants remain low-income and seek government assistance for their American-born children.

And yet the immigrants' perpetual struggle is to justify our existence to everyone around us by proving our economic value. We proclaim to be a nation that welcomes immigrants, but there are caveats for who those immigrants can be. Do you contribute to the economy? Did you come to the country legally? Do you use government assistance? Our parents, traumatized by the economic struggles in their home countries, constantly remind us that their sacrifice is a debt that must be paid off. In fighting to dispel the myth of the immigrant as a drain on the economy, we, too, put a monetary value on our lives. Too many of us have subscribed to the American myth that the people who work the hardest are the people who become the most successful.

I know this, and still I fight the urge to justify my existence by placing a price on it. I was on book tour at a political conference in the summer of 2017 when I met Ann Coulter. During one of the panel sessions, I heard her spew her anti-Latino rhetoric using data from hate groups like the Center for Immigration Studies. I'd seen her on Fox News and forced myself to read one of her books for research, but seeing the crowd cheer and applaud her made my chest contract.

I am not sure why I wanted to speak with her. Did I think I could change her mind about Mexican immigrants? Was I just trying to make a statement? She has written that there is "nothing good about diversity, other than the food, and we don't need 128 million Mexicans for the restaurants."[3] She writes comfortably about cultural appropriation, the taking of our culture, food, music, and language while discarding us, the people who produce it. To her, we are nothing more than the bones of a piece of meat that has been thoroughly consumed. That's how the idea of America has operated since its founding: it wants our land, our labor, our fruit, but not us.

White people love "Columbusiz[ing]," a word José R. Ralat calls in *American Tacos* "the term for Anglos 'discovering' something that is already a fixture in" a community that has been marginalized. Instead of recognizing these things have always existed and are part of American culture, white people will claim they "discovered it" and it's therefore theirs to claim.

Tacos, for example, have become as American as they

are Mexican. Though don't get it twisted, as Ralat told the *Los Angeles Times* "[Tacos] ultimately belong to Mexico. They get the final word."[4] We do. But now even Tucker Carlson has fought to claim tacos as American—what in his mind is separate from Mexicans and other Latinos. During an interview on his show, Carlson told Enrique Acevedo, a Univision news anchor at that time, that "[Tacos] are an American food." In the same segment, of course, he voiced his anti-immigrant sentiments saying how he's "totally opposed to illegal immigration . . . and our legal immigrations should be lower." White people will always want our culture, but not us, the people. But I digress.

Back to the story: While I posed with Coulter for a picture, I said, "Ann, I'd like to give you a copy of my book. It's my story of being undocumented, never being on any kind of welfare, and going to work on Wall Street."

It was the story that tagged me as a "good" immigrant.

She responded, "Oh, great. The two things I hate the most, illegals and Wall Street."

She took the book while a nervous smile flitted across my face and a knot of fire formed in my stomach. There aren't any facts, stories, or history lessons to help someone like her—she's a lost cause. She'll go to her grave a racist.

I wasn't angry with her—she proved to be exactly who she spells herself out to be in her many anti-immigrant books. I was irritated with myself because here I was, still using my precious time to engage with a racist on their terms. A chip remained on my shoulder. I wanted to prove to Coulter that I had earned my spot. I wanted her to know that I am a Mexican who had never used government assistance.

The truth, though, is that it's not about how much money I have earned. What offends people like Coulter is not the size of my bank account, but my Mexican body infiltrating what they believe should be a country for white people.

Nonetheless, in my attempt to make her see how wrong she is about immigrants, I walked through poisoned waters that reduce our lives to dollars and cents. By arguing that I deserved to be in this country because I had never been on welfare, I was inadvertently saying that those who have used government assistance aren't worthy. I do not believe that about other immigrants, so why did I believe it about myself?

I cringe thinking of all the times I've explained away my life with the economic output I produce. I once tweeted, then deleted, a copy of my 2007 W-2 that showed I had paid federal taxes when I still didn't have a green card. In 2014, the chief actuary of the Social Security Administration said that undocumented immigrants had paid over $100 billion into the Social Security Trust Fund over the last decade.[5] I wanted to show my contribution as if that money gave my life more value.

I understand why immigrant rights groups use economic

data to advocate for us. If the racists say immigrants are a drain, we must set the record straight. We pay taxes, we do jobs no one else wants to do. We keep the workforce alive, since U.S. birth rates are not keeping up with labor needs. Giving "Dreamers" a path to citizenship would add $799 billion to the GDP over ten years.[6] And the positive statistics go on. But our strategies cannot simply be the flip side of the coin. The majority of us don't go on to achieve what America says it wants from its immigrants—stories we can keep selling as proof the American dream is real and attainable. Stories we go on to use against immigrants, differentiating between the good, "successful" ones, and the rest.

There is a danger in perpetuating the image of the perfect immigrant, one who arrived with only pennies in her pocket and went on to become a millionaire. Yes, those stories are inspiring, and they should be celebrated. But they should not become the measuring stick for who deserves to be an American, because they set an intentionally unrealistic finish line. We cannot forget the many times we've shown our economic worth and still it hasn't rendered us worthy. Our lives have value because they do. We don't need a college degree, a six-figure-paying job, or a tax transcript to deserve the air we breathe. Our lives are worth more than money. Our reward has to be deeper than what's in our pockets. Our value to America has to be more than our labor. We are not here to give, we are here to be.

Disposable Scapegoats

My husband and I take frequent trips to Santa Barbara, California, where he grew up. The drive from Los Angeles along the Pacific Coast Highway is breathtaking. There are mountains on one side and the deep blue ocean on the other. About three-quarters of the way along, we sometimes see Latino farmworkers picking strawberries. Siempre se me escapa un suspiro. I never see their faces. They are bent down, with big hay hats protecting them from the sun and T-shirts around their necks. I think about their families, those they left behind, what crop they will tend to next. I wonder how many people drive by and see them as an interruption to their scenic view. I think about how many of them will be deported—only after they've left their soul on that field—and then be replaced by others who will continue to feed America.

Latino workers have kept the U.S. economy afloat time after time, but not even in the direst of circumstances has our labor made our lives matter. In the early 1900s, Mexican workers were actively recruited to come harvest the fields after the 1882 Chinese Exclusion Act left farm owners in desperate need of workers. We answered the call only to be blamed decades later. As the Great Depression pushed the United States into economic collapse, President Hoover saw the solution not in addressing the real economic issues, but in using Mexican Americans as scapegoats. To give white people the illusion of progress, as many as 1.8 million Mexicans, the majority of them U.S. citizens, were deported. Historians politely call the massive raids "Mexican Repatriation." But getting rid of Mexican workers didn't result in more jobs.

In the 1940s the Bracero Program was created to bring millions of Mexican workers back to the United States to help address labor shortages during World War II. They came to help, to keep the country running. And after they had stepped in, history repeated itself in the mid-1950s, when 1.3 million Mexicans and Mexican Americans were deported during Operation Wetback. But while President Eisenhower was disposing of our bodies as a solution to economic problems, he was also welcoming more European immigrants than had been previously allowed.

During the Covid-19 pandemic in 2020, many of the jobs undocumented people do—like picking fruits and vegetables, packaging the meat we consume, and even saving lives as first responders—were considered essential. A viral picture showed farmworkers during the pandemic harvesting crops while raging wildfires burned through the mountains behind them, the ashes on their faces. Many people hailed them as heroes. I am sure they would have given up their capes if it meant being able to stay safe at home with their families. Others just saw them as disposable illegals taking "American" jobs. But farm work has always been done by people of color: first the enslaved, then freed

Black people, Chinese, Filipinos, Mexicans, and other Latinos. There is no evidence that if wages were higher, white people would be lining up to take those jobs in the fields.

What better display of economic value is there than to keep the country running during a global pandemic? But still it wasn't enough. France isn't a perfect example of how to treat immigrants or people of color, but at least they offered fast-track naturalization to frontline workers, from the doctors to the cleaning ladies to the cashiers at grocery stores. The U.S. Congress refused to even include undocumented workers in the first Covid-19 relief package. Ron DeSantis, the Republican governor of Florida, imposed I.D. requirements for people who wanted to get immunized, because he said that he did not want people who "come from another country, or whatever," to have access to the vaccine. I'm not aware of him raising any objections about who picked the food he ate during the pandemic.

Unsurprisingly, Trump, marked by his obsession over borders and blaming everyone else for his failures, scapegoated immigrants for the Covid-19 pandemic. The virus was already spreading within the borders of the United States, but Trump's response was to pretend that the threat was alien and distant, calling it the "Wuhan" virus, the "China" virus, or the even more racist term, the "Kung-flu" virus. I knew that our progress toward containing the virus, saving lives, and preventing our economy from total collapse, for which immigrants would be blamed, could be measured in inverse proportion to the volume of his administration's racist propaganda.

As a country, we chronically forget how politicians, racists, and billionaires will blame any scarcity on the immigrant in order to hide their own culpability. The capitalist system, which is mired in free markets and competition, perpetuates a system of white supremacy because this benefits the bottom line. And it is killing us. Not just in poor working conditions, but in systemic health dangers. Diabetes today is the leading cause of death around the world. Mexico has one of the highest rates of obesity worldwide, but it wasn't always that way. The industrialization of food has changed our diets, our bodies, and our health. When the goal is to produce the most amount of food for the greatest profit, what is left is a decaying human body, dying faster than it should. When medicine is produced to line the pockets of investors, people who could be cured are left to die. It's easier to say the immigrants are bringing disease than to question how the health care system benefits from all of us remaining sick.

The U.S. government makes our lives legal or illegal to suit the financial needs of corporations. Nativists will scream, "America first!" as a pretense to protect "American" workers from the scary immigrant they see as the cause of their woes. They fail to see that we are all at the whim of U.S. corporate interests and foreign policy, which shape immigration patterns, and never for the benefit of the worker. Consider the NAFTA trade agreement, which caused so much controversy. The treaty between Mexico, the United States, and Canada didn't just hurt American workers. Mexican farmers, unable to compete with U.S. exports due to government subsidies, had to close their farms and cross to the United States to find work. Here, those workers became part of the cycle: their bodies were used to benefit factory owners and corporations; then the workers were deported and replaced, all while being demonized for problems caused by corporate greed.

As was true in the past, today's policies that favor the rich and punish the poor are made possible by the lies we tell. Immigrants aren't the reason the middle class in America is disappearing. We aren't the reason white working-class workers are out of jobs. Instead of looking at the Latino immigrant, we should follow the money. White people are taught that the undocumented immigrant is to blame for their fate, instead of questioning the factory owner, who is getting rich while they are getting laid off. As the number of American billionaires grows, the path to a comfortable life, to a house with a white picket fence, gets more and more difficult. The billionaire depends on workers remaining poor. We keep being fooled by the crumbs thrown at us without realizing there is a whole feast to be had.

If our collective lives are to be worth more than profits, if our bodies are to be treated as sacred, if we are to value the farmworker on the side of the road as much as we value the farm owner, we must understand how corporate greed benefits from white supremacy. There's always been a necessary nexus between the two. A necessary condition of slavery was that Black people be viewed as less than human. Essential to the colonization of Native peoples was that they be considered savages. Today, this country paints Latinos as racially inferior foreigners and continues to exploit us, deport us, and blame us for America's growing wealth inequality.

Still, the lie prevails because white working-class workers believe it. They have come to view their whiteness as more important than their hunger. They will often work against their own interests if that means maintaining their whiteness to keep people of color pinned to the ground. They should turn to the history of greed that killed their ancestors. European immigrants in the 1900s could expect to live an average of six years after arrival because of the harsh working conditions they endured under wealthy factory owners. White people must realize that they are being played, too, because while they enable the disposability of our bodies, they remain disposable, too.

Affirmative Action

I grew up believing that my responsibility as an immigrant was to give America more than it gave me—to be a "productive member of society." But my achievements weren't seen as something I worked for and earned. If immigrants remain poor, we are accused of laziness; if we become rich, well then, that was an opportunity we took from a "real" American. In either case we are viewed as thieves, taking from the government or the American people.

It wasn't affirmative action that got me into one of the top five undergraduate business school programs in the country. I graduated in the top 5 percent of my high school with decent SAT scores and an impressive list of extracurricular activities. More than 17,000 people apply to work at Goldman Sachs each year, according to *Bloomberg Businessweek*, and only about 300 land a full-time job. I graduated from college with honors, excelled at math, and knew how to network. I didn't get hired because someone felt sorry for me or needed to fill a quota, I landed the job because I had the skills. I am not suggesting that affirmative action programs are invalid, or that if someone benefited in college admissions or employment because of such policies, they are somehow less deserving. Quite the opposite. I believe affirmative action policies are antiracist and needed to bring about an equitable society in the United States. But our critics continue to maintain that we aren't smart or hardworking or qualified, and that the *only* reason we are admitted to Ivy League universities or land jobs at prestigious corporations is because of preferential treatment due to our race, ethnicity, and gender. Since when has it ever been advantageous to be a person of color in this country? So when I say, "It wasn't affirmative action. You worked for it. You earned. Own it," what I am saying is that diversity programs alone wouldn't lift us up without our hard work, talent, and intelligence. Affirmative action isn't a handout.

In 2014, Kwasi Enin, the son of two immigrant nurses from Ghana, was accepted to all eight Ivy League universities. In other words, a U.S. Black student ran the Ivy table. But his incredible accomplishment was reduced in the media to nothing more than affirmative action. "These immigrants, who arrived yesterday, will get affirmative action over white Americans. Do the media really not know how [he] got accepted . . . According to *New York* magazine, it's because he's 'better than you,'"[7] writes Ann Coulter. Kwasi was born in the United States, he didn't arrive yesterday. And yes, actually he is smarter than most of us.

The Supreme Court, in 1978, ruled that quotas based on race at public universities and other government establishments were unconstitutional. In 1996, California residents voted to strike down affirmative action policies and prohibit public universities from giving special treatment based on race, ethnicity, or sex. The law stands today after a reversal failed to pass in the 2020 election.

Still, some scream, *It's reverse racism!* believing affirmative action is a single law demanding that minorities, and women, be given preferential treatment. The extremist David Horowitz, in his book *Hating Whitey and Other*

Progressive Causes, calls the set of policies a "double standard for government-designated groups." These policies were born out of centuries of injustices toward people of color. But now they are viewed as discriminatory toward white people! We should be a race-blind society, Horowitz argues. However, not seeing color won't erase the gaps that centuries of inequality have created. There might not be government laws explicitly calling for the advancement of white people today, but there were plenty of them throughout history. Policies that, like compounding interest, helped white people grow their wealth exponentially.

According to the 2018 "Income and Poverty in the United States" report from the U.S. Census Bureau, the median income for white households is more than $29,000 higher than those of Black households and $19,000 higher than Hispanic households.[8] For women of color the wealth gap is even wider—Black women make 39 percent less than white men, Latinas 46 percent less. The wage gap between Latinas and white women is greater than that between white women and white men—that's how far behind we are. We earn nearly half, not because we work fewer hours, or are less smart, but because the view that Latinos are racially inferior outsiders continues to be passed down from generation to generation.

In 2019, Latino families held $36,000 in wealth compared to $188,200 held by white families.[9] Much of this is due to the disparity in homeownership: 73.3 percent of white people own their home, while only 47.1 percent of Latinos do. And our homes are worth less. When our families moved into white neighborhoods, they fled, and real estate prices went down. Now those same white families are moving back to gentrify our neighborhoods because they see an opportunity and are displacing us.

When we wonder why such huge wealth gaps exist in America, we have to look back at how the system was built to keep us behind. African Americans, Latinos, and immigrants of color have been systematically denied jobs throughout history. For example, Irish immigrants, "hungry and desperate, were willing to work for less than free persons of color, and it was no more than good capitalist sense to hire them," writes Noel Ignatiev. But when it was Black workers who were desperate and willing to work for pennies, he asks, why then "were they not hired to undercut the wages of the Irish, as sound business principles would dictate?"[10] We know the answer.

Later, when Irish immigrants faced dangerous working conditions and meager wages, they were able to organize, not only because there is power in collective bargaining, but because their whiteness allowed them to do so. The same cannot be said for Mexican immigrants. In 1917, a group of mostly Mexican miners belonging to the Industrial Workers of the World (IWW) walked out in protest for higher wages and better working conditions in Bisbee, Arizona—something that would have benefited white workers, too. But the strikes were broken by the Citizens' Protective League and the Workmen's Loyalty League, who called the strikers "traitors." The result was the illegal deportation of 1,876 IWW workers, who were put on railroad cattle cars and "dumped in the desert."[11]

Other immigrant groups such as the Chinese, who also faced deadly working conditions while building the railroads, were never able to organize for better working conditions. Their nonwhiteness prevented them from gaining labor protections, and even citizenship. In fact, once they started to become more financially successful by opening their own businesses, something that was celebrated within communities of white immigrants, they were banned from the United States.

The legacy of unions that kept African Americans, Latinos, Chinese, and others out of factory work—redlining, exclusionary immigration policies, the looting of Mexicans' land during the Mexican-American War, deportations of Mexicans during economic downturns—all created a gap that we are still trying to close. In a country where Black Americans have been viewed as "biologically inferior," Mexicans as "an ignorant 'hybrid race,'" and Chinese immigrants as the "ideal human mule," there is far from a fair chance to access the same economic opportunities as white people.

The story of how white people got ahead goes on, and yet, many still believe affirmative action policies today discriminate against them, when they've received every advantage to get ahead in the game. In college admissions, corporate employment, housing opportunities, access to credit, and everyday life, white people benefit from centuries of affirmative action on their behalf. White women are in fact the biggest beneficiaries of affirmative action programs in admission to academic institutions. Despite this, prospective student Abigail Fisher filed a lawsuit against my alma mater, the University of Texas at Austin, for denying her admission. At the time of her lawsuit, UT admitted the top 10 percent of each graduating public high school class regardless of race. Fisher graduated in the top 12 percent, but her lawyers argued that "even if she were rejected solely because of her grades and not her race, she could still claim a 'Constitutional injury' from being subjected to an unfair admissions process."[12]

If she only knew what discrimination *really* looks like. In 1975, the state of Texas allowed local school districts to deny public education to "foreign-born children" who were "not legally admitted" to the United States. It took only two years for the Tyler Independent School District, in East Texas, to charge tuition to students who could not prove that they were "legally admitted." A brave group of Mexican students brought a class-action lawsuit that was eventually won in the *Plyler v. Doe* Supreme Court case in 1982.

In corporate America, affirmative action for wealthy white people looks like nepotism, the uncles or grandfathers who can call in favors to hire their nephew or grandson. It shows up as the deals that are made on the golf course or at the strip club. I didn't row crew, play lacrosse or squash (I had to google "squash" as I wrote this to make sure it was spelled in the same way as the vegetable), as many of my colleagues at Goldman did—sports that say you are part of an elite group.

We do not live in a post-racial world simply because Barack Obama was elected president, or because Sonia Sotomayor serves on the Supreme Court. Affirmative action programs are necessary, not because minority candidates are not qualified, but because, left to their own devices, the people who hold the levers of power will always put the interest of white people first, even, and perhaps especially, at the expense of people of color.

Latinos make it to the top universities, hold prestigious jobs, climb the corporate ladder, and break glass ceilings all while jumping over hurdles, navigating unjust laws, and lacking the connections many wealthy white people benefit from. Yet we are the ones that feel like we don't belong in these spaces. We feel inadequate, as though we are not good enough to be there. If only we knew, we are better than good enough. Without any advantages, we still made it.

The Cost of a Dream

My husband, Fernando, and I became first-time homeowners in early 2021. In some ways, this house is the perfect bow that neatly ties up my American dream. It's proof that the dream is real and attainable. I am killing it.

Then I start thinking of the laws I've had to break. I reflect on all the manna that has fallen from above. If you don't believe in miracles, let's just call it luck. I cry when I think of the price I've had to pay for a healthy investment portfolio. For this house in one of the most expensive cities in the world. I wish I was certain it was all worth it.

My dad passed away in 2007. He lived in Mexico when I was still undocumented. If I got on a plane to be with him, to hold his hand as he took his last breath, I might not have been able to come back to the United States. I might have died trying to cross the desert like so many others. And even if I had a successful crossing, I'd be banned from applying to U.S. citizenship under current laws. So I stayed in my high-rise apartment in the Financial District.

I'll never be able to share tacos de aguacate, queso fresco y chicharrón, menudo on a hungover Sunday, or a Tecate with my dad. There isn't a day I don't wish I would have taken a flight to be with my father. Job, money, and America be damned. I believed in the American dream, but I didn't yet know how much it costs.

As my husband and I drove through South Los Angeles looking at houses, I thought about my mom. On a trip to Mexico a few months before, she told me she felt like a failure, because "What do I have to show for all the years I spent in the United States?" My parents didn't get to buy a home here, and they left the one they were building in Mexico unfinished when they first immigrated.

As she told me of the pain she felt because she didn't amass the fortune she dreamed of when she came to America, her eyes filled with tears, and though she would not release them, enough ran down my face for both of us. She said she was afraid of what would happen if she had let the tears flow.

I wish she felt what I feel. None of what I am, of what I have, would be possible without her. When I told her we were shopping for a house, she said, "Después de tanto sacrificio, te mereces eso y más." I told her, "Después de *tu* sacrifico. Esta casa también es tu logro." I remind her that the only reason I have what I have is because of everything she's given me, and of everything she's given up for herself.

This beautiful craftsman-style bungalow with fresh green grass, which apart from the light blue fence looks like one of those American Dream 1950s homes, was made possible by my parents, through their sacrifice, pain, and calloused hands. Their unfinished house in Mexico is the reason I can now buy one in the United States.

Then there is the flip side. The appearance of success requires children of immigrants to provide for our families, even as we struggle to make a life of our own. There is an unspoken rule in the Latino community that our parents will take care of us when we are young, and we will take care of our parents when they are old. This is part of the beautiful emphasis on family in our culture. My mom wishes she could make a lot of money and take me on vacation. She feels guilty because I am financially responsible for her. Her guilt is the biggest pain I feel: a constant knot that gets tighter every day. I became my brother's legal guardian when he was sixteen years old. I've lent money to my other siblings and stopped keeping count. Their debt has become my sin. *How can you possibly ask for the money back when God has blessed you with so much?* they ask.

The weight isn't a burden, but it is a heavy load to carry. I want to take care of my mom. I want to help my family. But family is supposed to be a mutual support system. When one person becomes an ATM for the entire family, when the help they expect is always financial, then beautiful values devolve into open wounds.

We're never supposed to talk about this in public, lest we be called "malagradecidos." We're also not supposed to talk about it in private, with a therapist, lest we be called "locos." The pattern continues. Our parents talk to us about the importance of hard work, but many of them don't talk to us about money.* They teach us the importance of

---

* A 2014 Wells Fargo Survey found that 55 percent of Latinos view their children as their retirement plan. The same survey found that while 92 percent of Latinos say their parents talked "a lot" about how important hard work is, "fewer

looking after our family, but not about taking care of ourselves. Many of us don't learn how to manage our money but are expected to be experts in provision.*[14]

I became the "successful" one in my family. My brother is on his way, but he's ten years younger than me. I am the one without children of my own. My other siblings have their own families to look after. "I made it" while others in my family have not been as lucky. My success becomes a judgment that they place on themselves—a judgment that somehow makes my success an insult to them.

I am expected to take care of everyone. Perhaps that's a pressure I have built up in my own mind. The guilt I feel when I spend the equivalent of my mom's monthly living expenses on a tempura dinner in Japan is of my own making. She's the most excited when I visit a new part of the world, commenting on my Instagram posts, "Eso te mereces, mi bonita."

I want to create boundaries that don't lace our sacrifice with guilt. I want to break the pattern. I want to help my children pay for college. I want to pay their first month's rent when they start their career. I know that's what my mom wanted for me. Life turned out differently. She worked so

---

than half reported that parents devoted much time to educating them about financial issues."

* A 2014 Prudential research study found that only 19 percent of Latinos had individual retirement accounts and only 10 percent invest in stocks.

hard all her life, but no one ever taught her about saving for a rainy day.

Fernando's mom sends us greeting cards for every occasion, Christmas and Saint Patrick's Day alike. On Valentine's Day 2021, she gave us a card along with a check to help with the furniture for the new house. I sobbed.

I do not know how an adult child-parent relationship works where the child isn't taking care of the parents. Jokingly, I said to Fernando as he told me "No llores, mi amor," that my reaction was because I thought only white people had this kind of relationship. Parents pay the bill when the family goes out to eat. They take care of the security deposit for their recently college graduated child's apartment. They have their own retirement accounts that hold stocks and bonds, not their children's dreams and ambitions. But clearly, some Latinos, like my husband, did learn this from their parents. Some Latinos who are undocumented open and manage successful businesses. Our Indigenous ancestors were experts in commerce. I've had to learn that respecting and loving myself sometimes means saying no to family without feeling as though the weight of a cement block has just fallen on my chest. I was nervous telling one of my family members about buying a new home. A few years ago, I drew a line in the sand and said no to taking out a mortgage so they could buy the house they were renting. When they saw a picture of my moving boxes, they asked if I was moving. When I said, "Yes! We haven't talked in a while. But we bought a house!" they never responded.

I went to therapy and realized I am not a bad immigrant for wanting America to see my human value before my financial potential, and I am not a bad person for wanting my family to love me even when I am not financially helping out.

What We Give Up

During a Netflix-and-chill Saturday during the pandemic, I watched the 1995 film *My Family (Mi familia)* for the first time. The classic Latino film follows a Mexican American family in Los Angeles through three generations, from the 1930s through the 1970s. The youngest child, Guillermo, known as Memo, is the "pride of the family." He's the one who went to college, became a lawyer, got out of el barrio, and became the most successful. He's also the one who changes his name from Guillermo to the English version, William, and goes by Bill. He's engaged to a pretty blonde, who assures her father and mother that Bill is not to blame for his family, you know those crazy Mexicans. Bill wears suits and has left East Los Angeles for a better life on the West Side.

When I imagined what Memo's movie spin-off would be like trying to play the part of Bill, I saw myself, and the false choices I was forced to make while trying to climb the corporate ladder—choosing between success and my culture. Many of us have viewed upward economic mobility as possible only outside of our community, and therefore through assimilation. So much of what we've learned points us in that direction. "Act professional" is just another way to say assimilate. Why are pearls professional and hoop earrings not so much? Who made up those rules and why are we still following them?

In *Bill: The Memo Story*, Memo would soon find out that his suit, new name, and apartment in the white neighborhood still aren't enough. Even with his new name, he'd never be able to shed enough of his Mexicanness to be accepted by his white colleagues and his wife's friends. Clients would still ask if he speaks English or ask his bosses for a different attorney. We'd want Memo to say, "Fuck it," and look for another job. But we'd also understand his desperation to fit in, because many of us have lived through it.

I know all too well what it is like to pretend. By the time I was twenty-four, I was an associate at Goldman, easily clearing six figures. I thought I had finally arrived. I had a college education. I talked like a white girl. I dressed in expensive Ralph Lauren suits. I had a successful career at the epicenter of our capitalist society. Capitalism and whiteness being co-conspirators, I believed that buying the things rich white people bought, like $6,500 Chanel purses or $1,000 Hermès belts, made me like them. But over time it became clear that even if I could absorb every aspect of America's elite society, that didn't magically make me a different person.

But things are starting to change because people of color are refusing to assimilate to make white people comfortable. We are realizing our success doesn't depend on their acceptance.

Hasan Minhaj (pronounced HA-sun MIN-haj), the American comedian and host of Netflix's *Patriot Act*, went on *The Ellen Show* in April 2019 and spent half his time on the air correcting Ellen DeGeneres on the pronunciation of his name.

"Hasaan Minaaj," Ellen said as she introduced him.

He said, "No."

Ellen responds, "Yes!"

Hasan says, "No."

Ellen says awkwardly, "No, really?"

Hasan then told the story of how when he started doing comedy, people in the business told him to change his name. He refused: "If you can pronounce Ansel Elgort, you can pronounce my name."

His father chastised him for using too much time to correct Ellen: "You wasted your chance."

"I think that's the big difference between our generation and our parents' generation. They're always trying to survive. And I mean survival is the thing, so just go by whatever she calls you . . . I think when Dad came in '82, he survived for us. But I'm trying to live. . . . So I'm gonna go on *Ellen*, the most American show ever, and make you hit all the syllables."

At a later appearance on his own show, Hasan shared that he went by "Sean" for two months, but that it didn't feel right. On his decision to spend half his time correcting Ellen on *The Ellen Show*, a huge platform with millions of viewers where he could have used his airtime to promote *Patriot Act*, he said, "I looked in the audience . . . [my mom] she kind of cringed . . . she gave me that name . . . And I'm like 'Dude, what am I doing?' I have a show with my fucking name on it and I'm still being like, 'It's with Sean'!"

In that moment, I felt so proud of Hasan, as if he was my longtime friend. He understood that with all his success, with his own hit TV show bearing his name, if he could not stand up and speak out, then when could he just be Hasan Minhaj, not some bland version that makes him digestible to white people?

There is so much power in owning the uniqueness of our names, our food, our heritage. Only when we refuse to change and instead recognize the beauty that has been passed down to us will we truly find acceptance within ourselves. We'll stop worrying that other people can't pronounce our names.

Uzoamaka Aduba, best known for her role as Suzanne "Crazy Eyes" Warren in *Orange Is the New Black*, has spoken about wanting to change her name when she was a child growing up in a mostly white town. "Nobody can pronounce it," she told her mother when she asked if she could go by Zoe.

Her mother responded, "If they can learn to say Tchaikovsky and Michelangelo and Dostoyevsky, they can learn to say Uzoamaka." And that's just the thing: if we can learn to pronounce their names, they can spend the time to say ours correctly, too.

Reflecting on not changing her name, even as she started her Hollywood career, Uzoamaka told a group of mostly Black and Brown girls, "What is amazing now standing in my womanhood, in my power, I wouldn't change my name for a second . . . so do not ever erase those identifiers that are held in you . . . it is yours . . . it is yours to own." The faces of the young girls lit up with smiles. Their nods suggested that some of them had probably picked up "nicknames" that were easier for their teachers or classmates to say, but now, listening to a powerful Black woman be proud of her name gave them permission to be proud of theirs.

I have recently added Natzely and Raya, my middle and married name, to my full name: Julissa Natzely Arce Raya. Natzely was too difficult for my white teachers to pronounce, so I let it go. It is a gift my parents gave me, meaning what I most love in Nahuatl, because they wanted me to know just how special I am to them. It's a present I rejected for twenty-six years for the sake of acceptance, to make white people comfortable. But not anymore. Now I make everyone say all my names.

We are finally seeing that success doesn't have to happen outside our community or in spite of our heritage. We are rejecting the notion that success is found in whiteness because that kind of thinking has never led us anywhere good. The antidote for the poison of the oppressor is to embrace our brownness, because it is our culture that is propelling us. Look at Bad Bunny, his El Último Tour del Mundo reached number one on the Billboard 200 chart—it was an *all*-Spanish-language album.

Becky G, accepting her Favorite Female Latin Artist award, said, "When I first got signed at fourteen, I did a cover and said, 'It all started when my grandpa crossed over / Now one day I'mma be a crossover.' It's insane because today I still carry that same sentiment, except I don't have to do the crossover because we are the crossover." And she is right: we no longer have to cross over to the English market, to the white market, to make it. Right where we are, we are more than enough.

My friend Patty Rodriguez tells a story about how her bilingual children's books were rejected by publishers because they believed Latino parents don't read to their children. She self-published and has sold over 1.5 million books worldwide. Not only that, but when raising capital to expand "Lil' Libros" she decided to make her customers, her community, owners in her company. She raised more than $1 million in twenty-four hours, and more than $2 million when it was all said and done. That's the power of our community!

This is the ending I'd write for my *Bill: The Memo Story* movie. He'd open his own practice in el barrio, teach his kids Spanish, and move back to the Eastside. He'd realize there is a different way to achieve success, one that is more rewarding. He'd reject whiteness and reclaim his roots.

Our lives are already a victory.

PART TWO
Embracing Our Truth

·4·

Reclaiming Our History

They've been telling us that all the success symbols are white and all the success symbols are gringos. And they've been denying us our culture, our history, and our contributions. We've been allowing it. We've been going over there and trying to act like somebody we are not.

—Rodolfo "Corky" Gonzales

We Were Here

On a Christmas trip to Mexico, I asked a few of my nephews who they imagined when I said "un americano." Without hesitation, they all gave me a similar answer: a tall white person with blond hair and green or blue eyes. Then I asked them, "What about Tío Julio, (my brother)? He was born in America—isn't he American? What about me? I am a U.S. citizen. Am I American?"

I don't blame them for the picture in their minds. Before I came to live in the United States, and for a long time after, I also thought that American meant white, and only white. Every American TV show I'd seen dubbed in

Spanish showed only beautiful rich white people. The self-image the United States presents to the world, through its leaders, its movies, and its history, makes it almost impossible to see anyone else as American.

I was confused, then, when the United States became my new home. In San Antonio, Texas, where I grew up, American culture was infused with Mexican customs, values, and flavors. Everyone, from the most Anglo to the recently arrived immigrant, crowded Mexican restaurants. Kids at my school looked like me, with brown skin and black hair. I heard Spanish being spoken almost every day at the grocery store, on the playground, and of course at home. The staples in the school cafeteria included corn dogs, but also cheese enchiladas. Kids of every background broke piñatas at their birthday parties—even when the theme wasn't a fiesta.

I was unsure of which American culture I needed to assimilate to. Was it the culture I experienced around me, or was it the culture I read about in my books and saw on my television or on school field trip to museums—the culture from which I was completely absent? The one that made me wonder where we were. I knew we, Mexicans, Latinos, existed, we were all around, but I felt invisible the moment I stepped outside my community.

As an elementary school student in Mexico, I read the history of Mexicans in what today is the United States. I later learned about the Indigenous and Black people left out of Mexican history books, too. In my new school I did not find any Mexicans in the story of the United States. Latinos have hundreds of years of history in this country. Where were our stories? "How did we become so goddamn nonexistent" asks John Leguizamo in *Latin History for Morons*. We have fought in every American war. Between 400,000 and 500,000 Latino soldiers fought in World War II. More than 80,000 Latinos served with distinction in Vietnam, many of them Puerto Ricans. As a percentage of their population, the island had more citizens fighting in that failed war than the rest of the nation.[1] Mexican Americans had the highest number of casualties.

Before and after there were British colonizers, there were the Apache, the Cherokee, and other tribal nations. A rich history tucked away in reservations, kept inside those imaginary borders. But in my American classroom, the stories were white: the independence from Britain, the founding fathers, the white heroes of the world wars. Even when we learned about slavery, emancipation, Jim Crow, and the civil rights movement, those stories were framed from a white point of view. We don't learn how Black people fought for their own freedom. Their sacrifices, organizing, and relentless determination has won every victory in pursuit of justice. We never learn about the efforts of African Americans to support Black Cubans in their war of independence from Spain. We learn that the United States is the pinnacle of democracy in the world, but how can freedom be made perfect when it was built upon the genocide of Indigenous people, the enslavement of Black people, and the colonization of Mexicans? What we don't learn is that the beacon of freedom, the inspiration for a true democracy for many, was Haiti, not the United States. Instead, children in American classrooms are taught that a white savior delivered Black people from bondage.

In his revisionist history, *An African American and Latinx History of the United States*, Paul Ortiz writes that one of his former students explained what it was like to learn the history of Black people: "How was I to regard my heritage with confidence while the environment I was raised in depicted Africans as nothing but slaves saved by a white man? Believe me, no teacher ever let me forget that."[2] When white people get to tell the whole story, what we are left with is lies, or at the very least a very incomplete picture. As congresswoman Alexandria Ocasio-Cortez told Maria Hinojosa in a *Latino USA* interview, "Our educational system largely teaches white people who they are and everyone else is a supporting character. And so if we really want to embrace who we are, it's kind of a tax in a way, because it wasn't given to us, we have to give that to ourselves." But sadly, not everyone is able to give themselves the knowledge, and so it is up to those of us who can to spread the word, the truth about who we are.

I was in the seventh grade when I first learned about slavery in the United States. When my dad picked me up from school that day, I cried recounting the day's lesson plan. I asked him, "Where were we?" We weren't Black, so we had not been enslaved, and we weren't white, so we had not been the masters. That question remained in my mind unanswered for a long time. I didn't have the words to describe how the racial dynamics in America made me feel like I didn't belong anywhere. I didn't know where Mexicans fell in conversations about discrimination, power, civil rights, or representation because the struggle, fight, and contributions of Mexicans and other Latinos were often missing from America's story entirely.

Mi mami and papi never talked to me about race or racism. It wasn't that they never experienced it. I saw my mom being followed in a store because the clerk thought she might steal something. I witnessed a white family leave the playground when my dad took my brother and me to run around. My immigrant parents just wanted to keep their head down, work hard, stay out of trouble, and achieve their American Dream. They didn't have the luxury of going to a library and reading books about Chicano history because they were too worried about providing for us. Without knowing who I was in America, without being grounded in my identity, I felt the pressure to assimilate into "mainstream" American culture, the one I read about in class and saw in the movies.

How can we see ourselves, how can anyone see us, when we aren't in the narrative—not in history, not in TV shows, not in the media, not anywhere. Growing up, I watched TV shows like *Beverly Hills 90210*, *Clarissa Explains It All*, *Friends*. There were no Brown Latino characters who looked like me and had stories like mine. *Saved by the Bell* starred Mario Lopez, but his name was A. C. Slater and it was not until *Saved by the Bell: The College Years*, that A. C. Slater "discovers" he is Chicano, and all that time Zach "just thought [Slater] was Italian." Now, having lived in the United States for nearly thirty years, I still don't see enough of us on TV. The hit TV show *Friday Night Lights*, one of my favorites, was set in a Texas high school. According to the Texas Education Agency, 52 percent of public-school students are Latinx. Yet the series featured only a single Latino character in its five seasons on the air—a troubled young man with anger issues who gets called a "wetback" by his classmate. In its tenth season, Showtime's *Shameless* finally had some Latino representation, but for most of their time on air, the Latino family was hiding from ICE, making tamales for three episodes. Then there is a "war" to protect their corner from another tamale-selling family. At one point in July 2020, there were zero shows on network TV with a Latino cast. In Hollywood films the representation is just as dismal. In 2019, according to the UCLA Hollywood Diversity Report, 67.3 percent of roles went to white actors, 15.7 percent to Black non-Latino actors, and 4.6 percent to Latinx actors, despite the fact that we purchase 23 percent of movie tickets.[3]

At some of the largest news outlets the number of Latino bylines is staggeringly low. According to a 2018 News Leaders Association survey, *The Washington Post*'s staff was only 4 percent Latino. *The Dallas Morning News* was 10 percent Hispanic in a city with a 42 percent Latinx population. The *Chicago Sun-Times*, 3 percent Latino when the city of Chicago boasts a 29 percent Latino population.[4]

In large parts of America, Latinos are seen just as foreigners and outsiders, mentioned only in the context of drugs, gangs, or immigration news. The "drug cartels," the "animals" of "MS-13," are often used to scare white people in the suburbs. But the people most frightened by narcos is us. They destroy our countries to satiate the endless drug consumption in the United States. The war on drugs is like any other war the United States has fought—never in white neighborhoods, the wreckage left for someone else to clean up.

We live in a country where there are more than 60 million Latinos, making up almost a fifth of the American population. But we aren't the ones narrating our own story; rather we became subjects at the mercy of someone else finding us worthy of taking up space in the world. Until our history, struggles, and unique experiences are unearthed, the whole country will suffer because the American story will remain incomplete. It's incredible what our people have survived in this country, and how little Americans of all races, ethnicities, and backgrounds know about it. When our rich past is kept from us, it leaves people to believe that we belong somewhere else—outside this country. Without an accurate telling of our history, we cannot fully address problems that are rooted in the past. When we are viewed as foreigners, our issues become someone else's problems—not America's problems.

The truth is that America is Latino is America. Like my parents, I am thankful for the opportunities I've had in the United States, but unlike them, that gratitude does not mean I am willing to just survive. I have removed the rose-colored glasses through which I once viewed America. I am creating a place for myself in this country that is my home. I used to believe that our liberation would be possible by getting others to see us as human, but now I recognize that *we* need to see us. We need to love us. We need to value each other. We need to give ourselves the gift of our history and heritage, nuestra herencia.

Remembering Those Taken from Us

We can no longer look away from the truth. We must take it upon ourselves to dig our stories out of darkness and into the light of justice. I wish I was a better poet, so I had pretty words and imagery to tell you about the faces and names of those who have fallen at the hands of white supremacy. But I don't have analogies to say fuck the police. It is not just la migra that hunts us. On June 18, 2020, Andrés Guardado, an eighteen-year-old Salvadoran American child, was shot and killed by a Los Angeles sheriff's deputy.[5] At the time of his killing, he had been working as a security guard at an auto body shop. His father, Cristóbal Guardado, told me Andrés was working two jobs to pay for his car and to help the family stay afloat after they took a financial hit due to Covid-19. The officers allege Andrés had a gun, but his family has repeatedly disputed the account. It wouldn't be the first time the police have planted a gun. According to the owner of the auto-body shop, any video evidence of what really transpired as Andrés ran down an alley, where the deputy shot him five times in the back, leaving two other graze wounds, was destroyed by the officers without a warrant.[6]

I have not stopped thinking about Andrés since the moment I saw his big bright smile in pictures circulating online. In him I saw my little brother, my young nephews, my future son. His life was just beginning. He had just graduated from high school. What happened to him still haunts me. I was heartbroken by how little attention Latino organizations initially paid to this injustice. His story didn't make national headlines. His name didn't trend on Twitter. Maybe that shouldn't matter because local organizations did organize and hosted vigils and protests. But I wanted everyone to care because it was a burden too heavy for us to carry alone.

Because the history of state-sanctioned police violence

against Latinos has been largely erased, it's easy to dismiss the deaths of Latinos at the hands of police as few and far between. But there are deep structural forces behind the violence waged against us. In the South, police had their roots as slave patrols targeting African Americans. In Texas, the Texas Rangers were formed in the 1820s as a racist, repressive, and violent force that rained terror on Mexicans and Native people as they cleared the way for westward expansion. They are painted as American heroes, almost mythical in stature. But from 1915 to 1920, up to 5,000 Mexicans "innocent of any crime but the one of being Mexican" were killed by the Texas Rangers.[7] The specific agencies may have changed over the years, but racist attitudes and actions in law enforcement have persisted.

The systems of policing and immigration enforcement are so corrupt and so rooted in white supremacy that they are beyond reforming. They must be abolished. It's not a matter of a few bad apples. In real life, when you take a bad apple and put it in a bowl with good apples, they all become rotten. The law enforcement system we have today is the rotten fruit of institutions that were created specifically to kill Black and Brown people with no accountability. The Los Angeles County Sheriff's Department (LASD) has for decades faced allegations that it is home to "deputy gangs" of white officers who work in primarily Black and Latino neighborhoods. In 1991, a federal judge described one such group as "a neo-Nazi, white-supremacist gang" and said higher-ups in the department "tacitly authorize deputies' unconstitutional behavior." We cannot simply make adjustments to such institutions, we must imagine completely new systems.

On June 2, 2020, twenty-two-year-old Sean Monterrosa was killed by a detective who shot five times through the windshield of an unmarked police vehicle. The Vallejo police chief said Sean was on his knees with his hands above his waist when he was killed by a detective who thought he saw a gun (it turned out to be a hammer). On June 6, 2020, California Highway Patrol officers in Oakland shot twenty-three-year-old Erik Salgado and his pregnant girlfriend, after shooting at their vehicle dozens of times. Erik died; his girlfriend survived but lost the baby. This was just in a three-week period.

In October 2013, Andy Lopez was thirteen when he was killed by a Sonoma County sheriff's deputy. Andy was walking through a vacant lot when the officer mistook his toy gun for an AK-47. He was shot seven times. In 2014, twenty-eight-year-old Alex Nieto was eating a burrito and chips at a San Francisco park when a passerby deemed him suspicious and urged his partner to call 911. Upon arriving, one officer unloaded his entire clip, then reloaded, shooting twenty-three rounds total at Alex. Another officer shot twenty times. Two more officers drew their guns and shot at least five times while Nieto lay on the ground dying. In a civil case against them, they claimed they thought the Taser he was carrying was a gun, and a jury found that they did not use excessive force.[8]

There is a severe lack of research and inadequate data collection of Latinos facing police violence since many states report race but not ethnicity of the victims of officer-involved shootings. However, the Raza Database Project found that between 2014 and early May 2021, at least 2,600 Latinos were killed by police. As of June 9, 2020, according to a database compiled by the *Los Angeles Times*, 465 Latinos had been killed by police since 2000 in Los Angeles County alone. The names of Latinos killed by the police go on and on, as was painfully clear at one of the Black Lives Matter protests I attended in July 2020. BLM Los Angeles shared space for Latino families to say the names of their loved ones who've been killed by police. It is thanks to the Black community's tireless work to increase police accountability and awareness, and its bold vision for defunding the police and imagining a system that serves the people, that the vicious killings of Latinos are starting to gain attention. This is the manifestation of "when Black lives matter, then all lives will matter."

As I researched the police killings of Latinos, I came across two stories that broke my heart and broke it again when I thought of how they've been kept from us. José "Joe" Campos Torres was a twenty-three-year-old Vietnam veteran who was beaten so violently by Houston Police officers on May 5, 1977 that it led to his death. Torres's body was found in the Buffalo Bayou days later. A rookie officer who was present during his torture said the two arresting officers threw Campos Torres into the water to see "if a wetback could swim." Joe survived war, but not the racist police. As for the killers, they were convicted of negligent homicide, sentenced to one year probation, and ordered to pay a $1 fine. Every time I've written killer, or killing, I've really wanted to write murder, or murderer, but I can't do that since none of these officers were convicted of murder, they hardly ever are. The Chicano community erupted in protests after the trial and carried signs that read "A Chicano's life is only worth a dollar." They fought back. They didn't stay silent.

The other story is more than a hundred years old. In the town of Porvenir, Texas, fifteen Mexican men and boys were abducted in the middle of the night, taken to a nearby hill overlooking a river, and shot by Texas Rangers from three feet away. All of them died. Without any proof, they were accused of being connected to a recent raid at the nearby Brite ranch.

The descendants of the Porvenir victims sought to memorialize the massacre with a historical market. They were met with resistance. The Presidio County Historical Commission chair called them "militant Hispanics," who had "turned this marker request into a political rally." Jim

White III, a descendent of the Brite family, told *The New York Times* that it was a "turbulent time on the border when you had a lot of people getting killed on both sides."

The families of those killed in Porvenir more than a hundred years ago did finally get their marker in 2018. Our stories must be dug out and shared because history not only tells us of the past, it informs our future. When we aren't aware of the pain of our past, we cannot know the magnitude of our fight. Today, we must tell the stories of those being killed at the hands of police. We must not allow their names to be forgotten because otherwise these injustices will be allowed to repeat themselves with no accountability. Our lives, our stories, they are worth more than a dollar. They are everything—worth all the gold, silver, and diamonds. Worth the moon, the sun, and stars. With our heads held high, and our eyes fixed on justice, we chant, we march, we fight.

What I Know Now

In April of 2019, I was invited to speak at my former middle school. For the first time in twenty-two years, I stepped onto the football field where I was first mesmerized by the clash of helmets, the breaking of a tackle, and the miracle of a Hail Mary.

I remembered what it was like to experience Friday-night lights in Texas, as a cheerleader on the field, to witness stadium lights swallow any hint of darkness, even on nights when the moon was resting and the stars were absent. The football field was transformed from scraggly brown grass with white ten-yard marks into peaceful green pastures that restored my soul. The students, parents, and retirees who filled the shabby metal bleachers in a 500-person stadium reverberated with the roar of the Colosseum itself. In Texas, football is everything. It's the only thing bigger than Texas.

This time I arrived not as an eleven-year-old girl, but as a bestselling author with a camera crew in tow because the local news station was doing a profile on me. As I stepped out of the reporter's black SUV, my knees buckled as memories of all the challenges I had faced while attending Mount Sacred Heart came flooding into my mind. The power of Friday night faded each Monday morning. I dreaded walking through the arched doors of the main entrance where mean kids waited to strike. Chants of "You don't even speak English," or "Her lunch smells funny," or "Why is her hair so long?" often greeted me when I arrived at school.

Before entering the building for my speech, I took a moment on the football field. I closed my eyes. The rustle under my feet reminded me of the whisper of the gold and maroon pompoms I once held, and of the power and confidence they gave me. I had become a cheerleader because of all the white girls I had seen in movies, thinking I, too, could become "all-American." I fantasized about what it would be like to be beautiful and white.

What I didn't know as a middle school girl was that long before I joined my squad, there were Chicana cheerleaders in Texas who were proud to be Mexican and who had fought for their right to cheer. Their stories weren't taught in school. My heart aches for all the things I learned too late. For the lost time I spent learning about someone else's pride when in our own community we have so much majesty to appreciate. Maybe if I'd learned their story, I, too, would have fought against the taunts instead of letting the pressure to assimilate take over my vocabulary, hair, and self-image.

In 1968, on a football field about a hundred miles southwest of San Antonio, a Mexican American student named Diana tried out for the cheerleading team. Many other Chicana students auditioned knowing full well that only one of them would get to cheer.[9]

The population of Crystal City, Texas, had been heavily Chicano for decades—by 1968 it was 85 percent Mexican American—but they had never posed a threat to the local systems of power. These citizens weren't denied the right to vote, but elections for city council and school board seats were conveniently held in the summer months, when most of the Mexican American families were away, chasing the harvests of sugar beets in North Dakota, cherries in Wisconsin, and tomatoes in Ohio.

Before the high school became majority Chicano, the students elected cheerleaders. But by 1968, the school was 87 percent Mexican American and the rules had to change. The school board modified the process so the mostly white faculty selected cheerleaders. Only one of the four cheerleading spots was open to a female student of Mexican descent. In a half-hearted attempt to mask their racist rules, they also added a requirement that cheerleaders must have at least one parent who graduated from high school. To this day, these types of institutionalized quota systems have fostered a mentality of scarcity among people of color. They fuel a culture of "there is only room for one of us." We've come to believe only one of us can access or hold on to a position of power, and as a consequence, we close the door on one another instead of fighting against the systems that create this dynamic.

Diana didn't make it onto the squad. She wasn't going to be on the field leading the crowd into cheers while the band played and the baton twirlers dazzled the audience with their performance. She wasn't going to decorate the football players' locker room during homecoming week. Her high school experience wasn't going to include the wonders of Friday-night lights.

Diana could perhaps try out again. But if she did, would she be betraying her community? After all, the pompoms she would be going after were those of her fellow Mexican classmate. There was an unspoken rule among Mexican students: no one would audition for the spot until the single Chicana cheerleader graduated. It was their way of showing solidarity in a school, and a town, where they were not wanted.

Diana was Mexican in a town that was described by *The New Yorker* as a place where "[the Anglos] had always been accustomed to leading the high-school cheers or anything else that was considered at all important to lead."[10] But 1968 was a year of reckoning in the United States. Communities of color all over the nation were rising up and demanding equality. In March of that year, 15,000 Latino high school students all across East Los Angeles staged a walkout to demand better education. That same month, over 1,000 Black students took over the administration building at Howard University, seeking to overturn racist policies implemented by the school board.

The Mexican American students of Crystal City High were becoming increasingly aware of the inequalities at their school and increasingly inspired by the civil rights movement around the country. Holding the pompoms might seem insignificant anywhere else, but in a small Texas town, there are few things more important than who snaps the football or who cheers on the boys. This was true in 1968, in 1994, and today. A fight for the right to cheer mattered. In the Lone Star State, it was an important indication of who was still in charge.

Reluctantly, Diana auditioned one more time. Once again, she didn't make the team. But this time, the students rallied around Diana's struggle and took their grievances to the superintendent of the school district. In the spring of 1969, Olivia "Libby" Serna, a senior, typed a list of demands, and along with a group of other students, took them to the principal. Among their demands was the abolition of the racist cheerleader quota system, freedom from repercussions for protesting for a better education, and the establishment of bilingual and bicultural education programs.

Diana Palacios told me on one of our phone conversations that the principal called the demands "baloney" and threw their typed list into a trash can. But the group of seniors did not give up. They took the demands to the superintendent, Diana added, who threatened to prevent the students from walking on graduation day if they didn't accept his "compromise." His solution was to have three Mexican and three White cheerleaders. Of course the superintendent's ruling didn't address the real issue: The school operated under an oppressive system for the majority of its student population. Still, this opened the door for Diana to audition a third time her junior year. She finally fulfilled her dream of cheering for her high school team. But her happiness didn't last long.

The white parents were embarrassed to take the three Chicanas on road games. Many of the other football teams in the district had only white cheerleaders. With very little resistance, the mostly white school board overturned the superintendent's decision in the summer of 1969.

Enough was enough. What started as a fight for the right to cheer evolved into something bigger. The Mexican students were tired of being physically assaulted for speaking Spanish in the hallways, of Mexican food being banned from the school's cafeteria, and of Mexican American history not being taught in school.

Three students—Severita Lara, Diana Serna, and Mario Trevino—among others, drew up a new petition with the help of Chicano activists José Ángel Gutiérrez and Luz Gutiérrez. The school board refused to meet with the students, but said they would meet with their parents, thinking that they would not show up for fear of being fired by their mostly white employers. Some parents were fired, but they showed up anyway. In fact the crowd was so large that parents had to stand outside and listen through an open window. The board reviewed the demands and said they found no basis of discrimination.

On December 8, 1969, the scales tipped. Over 2,000 students walked out of Crystal City High and its neighboring elementary and junior high schools. They held signs that read: "Brown legs are beautiful, too! We want Chicana cheerleaders." Camera crews descended on the small Texas town. Teachers from neighboring schools volunteered to teach the Chicano students during the walkouts at a community dance hall. The fight became a rallying cry for the entire community.

After seventeen days of school walkouts, the board relented and met the Chicano student demands: no more quotas for the cheerleaders, bilingual education, Chicano studies, Mexican food in the cafeteria, and more. The protests energized the entire Mexican American community of Crystal City to join the fight for liberation. Within two years, the school board and city council reflected the population of Crystal City, Texas.

The legacy of Diana and other Latina organizers has been lost as the decades pass. During the civil rights era, Mexicans attempted to create a place of their own in this country, but much of the Chicano movement has been forgotten, or the knowledge is available only to college students, or PhD candidates.

Though the Chicano movement was wildly imperfect, we continue to be barred from the knowledge of what happened and the lessons we could learn from both their victories, and their mistakes. In Arizona (formerly Mexican land), Mexican American studies were banned in 2010 until a federal judge permanently forbade the state from enforcing such laws in 2017. I didn't learn in my K-12 education about Crystal City, Texas, or the L.A. student walkouts, or the Chicano Moratorium, when over 20,000 protesters marched in East Los Angeles against the Vietnam War. I grew up thinking we didn't have a history in America, telling myself that books about us didn't exist because I hadn't come across them in my school. Both of these beliefs are false. The curriculum for the Mexican American Studies program in Arizona has an extensive list of books about the history and contributions of Mexicans. These are books the state of Arizona said caused "ethnic resentment."

As I have learned the real history, I've come to understand just how much Mexicans and other Latinos have withstood in this country. How we've been erased. How our struggles have been hidden, our student groups called anti-American. And I am resentful. But most important, I am inspired by their actions and the change they created.

It is with this sentiment that I walked into my old middle school. The principal greeted me inside the gym. It looked brighter, as if my cloud of sad memories had been lifted. I walked toward the stage, where a podium had been set up, and noticed the poster-sized pictures of my face lining the entire front wall.

One of the photos was of the 1997 MSH cheerleading team. My hair was down past my waist. It looked wild, like waves during a storm. We were doing a pyramid and I was holding a petite girl in the air with my bare hands. Anyone looking at these images would think

I had a wonderful middle school experience. I looked like a girl who fit in.

The other picture was my eighth-grade yearbook photo. I was smiling brightly, wearing a white blazer over a white blouse and a maroon necktie. My "Pocahontas" hair had been chopped off, and a flatiron had tamed it.

As I set up my PowerPoint presentation before the students arrived, I wondered how many of them felt like I did when I roamed those halls. How many of them wished their hair could be different, their skin lighter, their accent less obvious?

This was my opportunity to empower them, to make them hungry for more knowledge of their people. The students sitting in front of me were going to learn the story of Diana and Crystal City. And they were going to learn my story. I walked onstage proud to be Mexican. I had survived this place and the world beyond—even if it still has ways of reminding us who is in charge.

After my talk, the students asked me to sign the posters. They wanted to hang them in their bedrooms. I laughed inside, thinking how the pictures that hung on my bedroom walls during middle school were white Abercrombie & Fitch models because those were the faces of people I admired and wanted to imitate. And now my toasted almond skin, black hair, and dark eyes were what these young Latina girls wanted adorning their rooms.

Before I left the school, I went back to the football field. To the place that helped me survive. I snapped a selfie with the scoreboard that read "Home of the Mount Sacred Heart Eagles," and I did a little cheer.

For Diana. For me. For us.

·5·

Reclaiming Our Identity

my parents are Mexican who are not
to be confused with Mexican-Americans
or Chicanos. i am a Chicano from Chicago
which means i am a Mexican-American
with a fancy college degree & a few tattoos.
my parents are Mexican who are not
to be confused with Mexicans still living
in México. those Mexicans call themselves
mexicanos. white folks at parties call them
pobrecitos. American colleges call them
international students & diverse. my mom
was white in México & my dad was mestizo
& after they crossed the border they became
diverse. & minorities. & ethnic. & exotic.
but my parents call themselves mexicanos,
who, again, should not be confused for mexicanos
living in México.

—José Olivarez, "*Mexican American Disambiguation*"

We must start with how we see ourselves, not with how white America sees us. Reclaiming our identity is about addressing the battles within our community. About undoing and redoing. It is to stand in the middle of the storm, wet and naked, and to emerge in the sun clothed with a new vision for our future.

We speak different languages, have different skin tones, come from various socioeconomic backgrounds, hold varying religious beliefs. We view our racial identity differently. We are a rich and varied people, with different nationalities and distinct cultural, and ethnic backgrounds. In our home countries we are Colombian, Mexican, Honduran. Yet when we immigrate to the United States, we all become Latino. Some of our experiences are similar, like the trauma of learning to speak English, but others are not. White Latinos benefit from white privilege in a way the rest of us do not. Black Latinos face anti-Blackness and invisibility within our community. Indigenous people are often called Latino when many do not want to be—they already lost their identity once to colonization.

We are so distinct, in fact, that the very words we use to describe ourselves create debate within the community: Spanish, Hispanic, Latin, Latine, Latino, or Latinx are acceptable depending on who you ask, each word drawing its own support and criticism. In the United States, though, people incorrectly use these terms interchangeably to describe us as a monolith.

I used to refer to myself as Hispanic, but now I believe that doing so elevates the whiteness within our community and negates my Indigenous roots. Spanish is the language of our colonizer, the one that replaced our native Indigenous tongues in many places. It should be noted that hundreds of Indigenous languages are still spoken in Latin America and in the United States. We've made Spanish our own, creating words and re-creating language. Dominican Spanish is different from Mexican Spanish, which is different from Guatemalan Spanish. The people from Spain are European and are often white.* Hispanic is supposed to describe those connected to Spain, or people who speak Spanish and have roots in Latin America.

People from Spain are Hispanic, but they are not Latino or Latina, a word I use to describe myself now. Some of my Spanish friends have made their case as to why they are Latino, but I still don't think they are. I love them, but I don't see them as people of color. Latino is defined as a person whose origins are in Latin America, or who have ancestors from Latin America. The linguistic roots of the word aside, Latino was a term invented in the United States. It's not about who is "Latin," as in the Romance language, by which reasoning then Italians would be Latino, and who would make that case?

Latinx has recently come into popularity as the most inclusive term because of its gender neutrality—though it attracts criticism for being elitist and accessible only to people with college degrees. Others view it as further

* Because Spain was occupied by the Moors, not all Spanish people are white.

colonization, as forcing Spanish to be like English. I am not sure what we collectively should be called, nor is it up to me, but I do know that we are not the monolith America paints us as. Yes, each label has its shortcomings, but each also holds a truth about who we are, and how we came to be. Our history is messy, our people scattered, our national, political, and racial stories a web that makes us strong and also leaves us caught on sticky silk.

The variety of our labels is matched by the diversity of our skin tones. Many people don't imagine a woman with fair skin or blond hair when thinking of a Latina. As I discussed in part one, there are hierarchies according to skin color in Mexico and other Latin American countries, which place white people at the top. A term has developed in the United States to say some Latinos are "white passing," but I am not sure what it means to pass as white. Doesn't that just mean someone *is* white? Crossing the border to the United States doesn't change a person's skin color or the power that whiteness affords them.

And still, white skin doesn't make a Mexican or a Honduran or a Colombian any less Latino. They are still viewed as ethnically different, they still experience ethnic racism. If you speak with an accent or have a Spanish last name, things are more difficult in America, there is no denying that. But those who are white walk through the world without being denied humanity on the basis of their skin color.

I have a friend with hazel eyes. If it wasn't for her name, people would see her as white. She told me that she doesn't consider herself white. Whiteness has always felt foreign to her. In her school, the white kids exhibited a confidence she did not. They played water polo, popped prescription pills, and watched movies she'd never heard of. She told me that she felt out of place not because of her skin tone, but because she didn't have the wealth they did. While race and class intersect, one does not negate the other. She asked me, "In your view, is whiteness mostly about skin color, about your dominant genetics, in my case European, or is it also about a point of view—about psychologically and philosophically embodying whiteness?"

I responded that whiteness is a cancer. People who aren't white are capable of advancing whiteness, too. Yes, whiteness and being white are different concepts, but in Mexico she'd be "blanca," and coming to America doesn't change that. If a scholarship for Indigenous Mexicans existed in Mexico, a white Mexican wouldn't be eligible, but here in the United States, when we are all labeled Latino, the same distinction doesn't apply. I do take issue with the fact that in every area of American life, white people hire white Latinos to be able to pat themselves on the back and claim "diversity." This, I must say, isn't progress.

In a text, my friend José wrote to me: "I want white Latinos to be mindful that the stakes are different for them. They're less likely to be recognized as Latinos, but they are also less likely to be pulled over by the police. But I think there is potential in asking white Latinos to renounce their allegiances to whiteness. To embrace Latinidad and fight for justice."

I think part of that renunciation has to be a full recognition of how the experiences of white Latinos are different. I've found many white Latinos to be hesitant to call themselves white, to stop short of fully confronting the advantages their white skin affords them. I should also say that it's not only white Latinos who should renounce whiteness, because there are plenty of Black and Brown Latinos who aspire to it, too. I was one of them once. I also think we are pushing, guilting, lighter-skinned Brown Latinos to identify as white when they aren't. I've seen several people say they are no longer identifying as people of color, and certainly white Latinos could take note, but when I look at them, I can't see anything other than their brownness. We are rightly pushing the community to confront the racism within, but there isn't a planet in the universe, in which Selena Quintanilla (may she rest in peace) would be considered white, or hold the privileges of whiteness, and yet that's the argument some people are making. Isn't the purpose of this reckoning with our identity to create more space, to be more inclusive, to recenter the power dynamics? But sometimes it feels like the conversation has moved into a binary where only white Latinos and Black Latinos have stakes in the conversation. Someone like me who doesn't fit into this dynamic is left in the overflow room, despite the fact that my existence plays into all of it.

We have to unpack how the Latino identity was formed, who it serves, and what purposes it advances to heal the wounds and come together as an inclusive community. We have to face the fact that a Latino doesn't exist without the violence, rape, and genocide of Indigenous peoples carried out by European colonizers. A Latino doesn't take shape without the brutal history of slavery. The transatlantic slave trade didn't have the United States as its only destination. In fact, more than 90 percent of enslaved Africans were taken to the Caribbean and South America.[1] The history of how we came to be a mixed people, how we came to be Latino, is an ugly one of colonization, genocide, and slavery. This violent mixing is like a cosmic explosion—it leaves me in awe and in terror.

What's left of colonization is a continued denial of the existence of Latin Americans' African roots, a belittling of our Indigenous past, and the negation of our Indigenous present. People from Brazil to Mexico have continued to try to "whiten" the race. This isn't just some deep-seated anti-Black racism or rejection of one's indigeneity, but a way that colonized people could move up in the caste system set up by the Spanish and Portuguese. To marry someone European or a light-skinned mestizo meant a better life. But what we have to realize is that whiteness has never offered us safety. The official system is gone, but its seeds have been carried in the wind through generations. These seeds are constantly evolving, growing new roots that flower a different type of caste system, creeping into our conversations and becoming less easy to spot.

Debate has raged among Latinos as to whether or not a "Latino" community should exist at all—that the community is beyond repair. The anti-Blackness is a weed that keeps coming back because we've been unwilling to dig deep enough to pull out its roots. The anti-Indigenous sentiment is often completely ignored. The poet and interdisciplinary artist Alán Pelaez Lopez, who identifies as AfroIndigenous, created the hashtag #Latinidadiscancelled, a "critique" among other things of the "ways in which U.S. Latinidad has created an ideal Latinx citizen: white & white mestize, cis [gender, heterosexual], thin, normatively attractive, able-bodied, and 'respectable.'"

I understand why Black Latinos have called for the cancellation of Latinidad, for the community has denied their existence. Because I grew up in Texas, my own understanding of Latinos was narrowly shaped by those around me—Mexican and Brown. When I moved to New York after college, my Latino experience became fuller, more vibrant and complete. And then I moved to Los Angeles, where our communities are largely segregated. Pelaez Lopez started the movement after they moved from the East Coast, where they said there was room for Blackness within the Latino community, to California, where other Latinos refused to speak to them in Spanish. L.A. Mexicans, they said, "are not my people." And yet, they are somebody's people.

The boundaries that define communities are often artificial, put in place by categories forced on us by white America. There is only one way to be Latina, one way to be Black, but somehow many ways to be white. In a conversation with Blactina founder Nydia Simone, Pelaez Lopez discussed how growing up in Mexico they knew they were different, but they didn't always know they were Black: "the only way to be Black was to be African American." The word Black has "always meant African American," Simone agreed.[2] In *How to Be an Antiracist*, Ibram X. Kendi writes about how some African Americans were "wary" of the increase in the Black immigrant population, which has tripled since the 1980s. He writes: "I was African American, at a time when Haitian immigrants were feeling the sting of African American bigotry." White people weaponize immigrants against native-born Americans, and in the same way they pitted Black Americans against Black immigrants. We must recognize that the "racist ideas we consume about others come from the same restaurant and the same cook who used the same ingredients to make different degrading dishes for us all," Kendi says.[3] But things are changing as Black people push against a one-dimensional understanding of Blackness.

In September 2019, *The Root* released a video called

"Breaking Down the Anti-Blackness of Latinidad," where the host, Felice León, discussed the historical roots of racism in Latin America, pointing out that those sentiments are still alive today.[4] I nodded my head as she touched on how whiteness is centered in our community. The piece was packed with facts and historical analysis. It also called for the canceling of Latinidad. It said that so many Black and Indigenous millennials of Latin American descent were moving away from the term in part because when people imagine what a Latina looks like, they think of Jennifer Lopez or Penélope Cruz. León asked one of her guests, Janel Martinez, the founder of the blog Ain't I Latina? how she chose to identify herself. "I personally chose to identify myself as a Black woman, first and foremost," she said. She's gone by Afro-Latina in the past, but her sentiments have shifted as she centers her Blackness more and more. Latinidad, she said, "serves a very narrow audience."

I wondered if I was inside or outside that narrow audience. I look like neither JLo nor Cruz. I am a brown-skinned Indigenous woman. "To be Latino is to have a distance from Blackness and indigeneity," author Palaez Lopez has said. I cannot separate my Indigenous roots from my being; they are who I am, and the way others see me, too. I am not a white Latina, not visibly, not in any way. But because I am not a Black Latina, I have privileges because society still regards Black bodies as the most dangerous ones. I am Indigenous, but also not Indigenous.

My blood is Indigenous, and some friends have suggested that we should reclaim our indigeneity. But aren't we then co-opting an experience we have never lived through? I did not grow up in an Indigenous community, and therefore I did not face the same discrimination as Indigenous people. I embrace my Indigenous roots, but learning about the culture, the traditions, and the healing practices, or even learning Nahuatl, Tepehuán, or Huichol, doesn't make my life the same as that of Indigenous people who've been oppressed in a very different way. Identifying as Mexican, as Latina, does not come from trying to hide my Indigenous roots; it comes from a deep respect for Indigenous people and what they have endured. It's not about separating myself, but about confronting the privileges that I possess.

For years, questions about where I belong within and outside Latinidad and how to love myself when my identity is so nebulous swirled in my mind. Settler colonialism, critical race theory, and other phrases used in critiques of Latinidad were not concepts I understood when I first encountered them. I had only my experiences, not the language to fully describe them yet.

The Latino carries in us the generational trauma of our ancestors, the push and pull of keeping our traditions while assimilating to the colonial powers for survival. Maybe the Latino culture is the result of settler colonialism. Maybe ours is a culture that continues to erase Indigenous cultures even though it's been a long time since the colonial powers officially left. Maybe our minds are still colonized. In many ways, having a single identity that pulls white, Black, Indigenous, and mestizo people together under a single term feels like another form of mestizaje—partly the fabrication that we can mix enough to become a new people, thus erasing our Indigenous and Black roots. Though today to say I am mestiza is to say I am not white. To say I am mestiza is to assert my Indigenous roots and to name the violence of colonizers exerted upon my Indigenous ancestors.

For much of my life, I never felt rooted anywhere. I didn't fit in the "American" white or "American" Black narratives. I heard a story of a famous Black intellectual telling a Brown Latino that he didn't have a place in conversations about race in America. I believe he was and is wrong. Latinos, Black, Brown, and Indigenous people must all have a place in conversations about race. Latinos are deeply examining the racial construct of our own identity, how anti-Blackness permeates our community. We cannot look beyond the oppression of Black people in America or within the Latino community. Theirs has been the principal struggle that defines race relations around the world, and particularly in an America that was built on their enslavement.

White supremacy doesn't stay alive just because white people subscribe to the idea of white as superior. It has required a white-over-Black racial dynamic that pushes people of color to hide their nonwhiteness, and by doing so, keeps us at each other's throats. We must stop doing the work of white supremacy. Part of that labor is breaking the binary that drives people to seek whiteness when we should be seeking our own identity. We must all examine our role in white supremacy and fight against the violence it brings upon our people. There is space for all of us to be part of the solution. In fact, I believe it is the only way.

In the summer of 2020, Latinos were dying at much higher rates from Covid-19 than white Americans. We had some of the highest unemployment rates, since many service jobs are held by Latinos. The news coverage largely ignored these facts. I tweeted out: "America doesn't care about Latinos. We're still seen as foreigners, as someone else's problem despite the fact that the first Mexicans got here before the Mayflower." A reader responded: "There have been millions of Americans who've come out (me included) and supported immigrants of all kinds . . . you know who has experienced [discrimination] for even longer than anyone? African Americans." These two statements should not be in opposition. My point had been that all Latinos are viewed as immigrants—something the responder overlooked when he said that he supports Latinos by supporting immigrants. I'll say it again: not all Latinos are immigrants. Some were born here. Some of us are immigrants who have lived our entire lives in America. Others just arrived, but none of us deserve to be seen as alien. All of us deserve a place to belong.

Where I once sought whiteness to belong, with Latinos of all backgrounds I found a home—a place to be held, to unite, to be proud. I have found belonging with the Mexicans and Colombians in Texas, the Dominicans and Puerto Ricans in New York, the Salvadorans in Los Angeles—the three places in the United States where I have lived. It was in the company of Latinos that I let go of my assimilated self. When I couldn't see myself in "American" culture, I knew we existed, thrived, and mattered because our community showed me that we did. I craved that feeling of authenticity more and more as I grew closer to our community. I learned to carry all of me everywhere I went because of all the Latinos I met who were fully themselves everywhere they went. Among us, I could laugh loudly and dance joyfully. I didn't have to explain, I could just be. Whether it was during college meetings for the Hispanic Business Student Association, dancing in the Dominican clubs in Washington Heights, or during late-night dinners at Korean barbecue places with Mexicans in entertainment in Los Angeles, we've created space for ourselves. When America denied our existence, we said, we are here.

Embracing my Latina identity for me has been a form of resistance. But I do question what parts of me erase others; how in my quest to belong, I may exclude someone else. We are all trying to make space for our lives and experiences in this crazy world. It's painful to know that where I have found belonging, others have been rejected. It is with that understanding that I cannot write about what it means to be Latinx or Latino or Hispanic. That would be like asking what it means to be American. And who can define it for the rest of us? No one person can or indeed should. As it relates to the Latino identity, I have more questions than answers. People have spent decades studying our identity: what it means, and what connects us all under a single term. Is it enjoying a similar culture, speaking the Spanish language, having been colonized by the Europeans, having roots south of the United States and in the Caribbean? It's at once all of those things and none of them.

What I do know about Latinos is that the decisions of the past, conscious or not, about whether to be accepted as white or to reject that some are white have created deep fractures within our community and in our interactions with other marginalized groups. Fractures we must tend to if we are really going to be co-conspirators in the fight for justice.

Being Latino is complicated, at times contradictory, but it's also beautiful. I still believe that we can reclaim, reframe, and redefine what it means to be Latina to include all of us. I still very much believe that there is power in uniting as a Latino community. I believe that if we stopped seeing one another as the enemy, if we helped build one another up, instead of tearing each other down, we'd create real power for our community. Power that doesn't center on whiteness but on our full authentic selves.

What Is My Race?

Latinx and Asian and African and European and Indigenous and Middle Eastern: These six races—at least in the American context—are fundamentally power identities, because race is fundamentally a power construct of blended differences that lives socially.

—IBRAM X. KENDI, *How to Be an Antiracist*

When I was about fourteen, I went to the doctor, after my mom had tried all her home remedies to cure me first. We must have gone through two bottles of VapoRub. As I was filling out the paperwork, I asked her, "¿Mami, cuál es mi raza?" Confused, she said, "Eres Mexicana." I told her that Mexican wasn't an option; there was Black, Asian, Native American, or White. "I guess put white, then," she said.

I could read into my mom's choice to circle white, but that wasn't her first instinct. She had wanted me to check Mexican, because we are raza. My identity as a Mexican fills my mind and heart with my culture, and it also surrounds and enters my body as a racial marker. As a Mexican, as a Latina, I am racialized because "all ethnic groups, once they fall under the gaze and power of race makers, become racialized," writes Ibram X. Kendi. Yet my racial identity is a concept that escapes intellectual conversations about race. My personal experiences contradict the idea that Latino is only an ethnicity and not a race.

But suggesting that Latino should be a race confounds the situation even more, because we are all so different and experience the world differently, though the same could be said of any other racial group.

When others state, "Latino is not a race, it's an ethnicity," they ignore that not all Latinos have the same ethnicity, either. And though we don't all share the same ethnicity, the exact language, religion, customs, culture, food, and so forth, and though we are not the only ethnic group in America, we are the only people who are singled out by our ethnicity. Take the U.S. Census as an example. Everyone who fills it out has to answer if they are "Latino/Hispanic/Spanish" or not. If the following applies to you, check the box, the instructions read: "Hispanic origin can be viewed as the heritage, nationality, lineage, *or country of birth of the person or the person's parents or ancestors before arriving in the United States* [italics are mine]. People who identify as Hispanic, Latino, or Spanish may be any race."

Why are we specifically called out as needing to identify ourselves as "before arriving in the United States," when according to the Pew Research Center, 67 percent of U.S. "Hispanics" are U.S. born? And what of the Mexican Americans whose ancestors have always been in the United States, who never crossed the border? What about Puerto Ricans who've never been immigrants and whose forefathers may have never left the island? Every time we check that box, it separates us further from the American consciousness. Each time a non-Latino person reads that sentence, it cements into their mind that Latinos are from somewhere else—that we belong someplace else, that we are un-American.

And if our heritage, our culture, our customs, are separate from those of America, how can we ever truly be seen as what we are: a critical and important part of this nation? As Latinos, we have beautiful and distinct cultures that should be preserved and passed on to future generations. At the same time, American culture is Latino culture. Without our influence, America would have less texture, rhythm, flavor. In framing us this way, we are made into perpetual aliens.

We came to be considered an ethnicity because the Immigration and Naturalization Service (the former office of immigration before the Department of Homeland Security was created) and the Census Bureau decided to categorize us as such. When I first learned this, I had to let the information marinate for a minute. Why would immigration want to label us foreign, if not to deport us and always hold us as the invaders? There was also lobbying by African American, Native American, and Asian American civil leaders for Latinos to be classified as an ethnicity because they feared lower representation for their own racial groups.[5] But that's more of white supremacy's power, leaving people of color to fight for the scraps.

Many intellectuals argue that race is a social construct, meaning that we, as a society, give it meaning. Race doesn't tell us about society—society tells us about race. Society has already made it clear that Latinos are seen as a race—we experience discrimination because we are seen as racially different. If the definitions of race and ethnicity are constructed and deconstructed by those in power, why can't we reframe Latino as a race to better understand where we fit in America's racial framework in America? Isn't Latino a mixed race, even by the way we currently define race? Race is not biological. It is political and personal. To have a Latino race is not to say we are all the same but that we are organizing ourselves politically, to be counted accurately, to garner political power for the benefit of our entire community. To not be erased.

It would not be the first time that racial categories have changed. In 1888, there were sixty-three racial categories, and in 1924, there were twenty-nine.[6] Mexicans were once considered a race on the U.S. census—in 1930. The addition of the "Mexican" race category came during the Great Depression and perhaps helped to identify and deport millions of Mexicans, even if they were U.S. citizens. As a result of these atrocious actions, Mexican elites, and activists, pressured the Census Bureau to label us as "white" as a form of protection, but as is true of other times we have sought shelter in whiteness, it didn't keep us safe.

It wasn't until the 1960 census that we were counted again, when five southwestern states reported on "white persons of Spanish Surname." In 1970, the question of

"Hispanic" origin was added to the long form after Latino civil rights organizations, activists, and others pushed for this. But not every household filled out that section, and the question was worded so poorly that we were grossly undercounted. This is important: in advocating for a "Hispanic" category, we were asserting that we were not white, because before this we were lumped in with white people. Even if it fell short, this is what put us on the map, how we said "We are here, we are different, and we want to count."

Our categorization matters—it makes us visible in this country we have contributed so much to. In the 1960s and 1970s, we were not considered a minority, and therefore we were not viewed as needing civil rights protections. In fact, it wasn't until 1954, after the Supreme Court case *Hernandez v. Texas*, that the Equal Protection Clause was extended to non-Black communities, at least on paper. At last, in the 1980 census, the question of Hispanic *ethnicity* was added to the short form, asking, "Is this person of Spanish/Hispanic origin or descent?"

In the 2020 census, there were thirteen choices for race: White, Black or African American, American Indian or Alaska Native, Chinese, Filipino, Asian Indian, Vietnamese, Korean, Japanese, other Asian, Samoan, Chamorro, other Pacific Islander, and "some other race." The "white" category is the only one that doesn't need any further classification. Filling out these types of questionnaires hasn't gotten easier since that time at the doctor with my mom.

I've hesitated in the past to check "Native American," because it's usually meant for people enrolled in a tribe in the United States. This time, because the census named Maya and Aztec as eligible tribes, I checked the box, along with all the other boxes from my 23andMe results, which show that I am 76.9 percent East Asian and Indigenous American (with roots in Mexico, Central, and South America), 18.8 percent European (mostly Spanish and Portuguese), and 2.0 percent sub-Saharan African. I didn't need a DNA test to tell me I am Indigenous—I wear it proudly on my face—but I was glad to have this information when filling out the 2020 census.

Submitting my DNA to 23andMe was a privilege many others didn't have access to. I wondered how other Latinos count themselves in terms of race. I was curious to find out. I posed a query on my Instagram account: "What did you choose as race on the Census?"

"I was born in Colombia, adopted by white parents, I think I put white," said one respondent. Another said, "I hated [this question]. I put white . . . But I sat there for a while thinking about how fucked up this is!" Someone else felt the same way I did when I was a young girl, "I never feel right choosing 'white.' But what else do I choose!"

Julie Dowling, author of *Mexican Americans and the Question of Race*, told NPR: "About half of Latinos who checked white on the census, a very nominal amount of them thought of themselves as white." The reason they checked "white," they said, is because "I don't fit anywhere else. There's nothing else to put." This is not to negate the fact that as I previously mentioned, there are those Latinos who are actually white.

In the 2000 census, the Census Bureau reported that of those who identified as Hispanic, 92 percent were white. But that's not really true; 42 percent of Hispanics chose "some other race," 48 percent selected "white," 2 percent selected "Black," and 1 percent selected "American Indian."

Dr. Laura E. Gómez calls it "perverse" that the Census Bureau would disregard our preferences and combine, with little explanation, the percentage of those selecting "some other race" and those selecting "white." This narrative matters. If the reported number is simply "92 percent of Hispanics consider themselves white," that sends a message of how we view ourselves—as still aspiring to whiteness.

For some, it *is* telling of how they've assimilated into whiteness. The Latino men who selected "white" as their race in the 2000 census are older, unemployment is lower, they are more likely to be Republicans, earn more money, have higher education, and be registered to vote. What this says to me is that some Latinos still equate success with whiteness. But the truth is much more nuanced. Since the 1980s, the percentage of Latinos who chose "white" as their race has decreased from 64 percent to 48 percent. The 2020 Census provided even more proof that as a community we are rejecting whiteness. The number of

Latinos who identified as "white" in the racial category decreased by 53 percent, bringing the total number of Latinos who identify as white to 20 percent.

The census isn't the be-all and end-all, and counting us more accurately won't make our place in America any less difficult. But it does matter. The census is important for federal funding into our neighborhoods, congressional representation, and upholding civil rights laws. The data is also used widely to study the makeup of the United States, population trends, and so much more. The census is just one example of how Latinos are erased in America. It is emblematic of a larger system that keeps our history and contributions hidden from us and from the millions of other Americans. There is still no uniform way to count us. And if statistics don't accurately reflect us, how then can we truly know how deeply we are affected by issues of policing, education, employment, lending, and so forth?

Ultimately, race doesn't tell us a person's spiritual beliefs or political ideology. It is a poor descriptor, but it is an important way to be counted. In this regard, I do believe Latinos, despite our many differences, can find power in numbers if we are counted as a race. The community is also saying this, as evidenced in the 2020 Census; 42.2 percent of Latinos chose "other" as our race. I believe that "other" is a call to have Latino be a racial category. Conflicts within our community notwithstanding, I remain hopeful that as Latinos we can come together to fight for our rightful place in this country.

·6·

Reclaiming Our Culture

We Don't Need a Translator

As a writer, I am constantly asked to make my stories more relevant, but relevant to whom? To make them more appealing to a "mainstream" audience, and I know that's not coded language for larger, it's coded language for a white audience. To make them less angry, but it's not anger in my words, it is truth. All I want to do is write stories that make sense to people like me, people who have had to answer a million questions just to make others comfortable. Freedom from the white gaze is what I desire. I don't want to translate my experiences so they make sense to other people. I want to write about heroes that look like us, speak like us, and triumph despite every possible challenge they face. People whose humanity is recognized without the white stamp of approval.

It's true that not every one of my pieces is going to fit every publication. It's also true that publishing houses, newspapers, magazines, and journals have been built on a resounding white male voice.

The year 2020 was marked by a global pandemic, and it is a year none of us will forget. If you are a Latina writer, there is another reason why 2020 was a year of reckoning: *American Dirt*. The book, which was published by Flatiron Books (the same publisher responsible for this book), was a painful reminder that our real-life experiences are important only when they are packed with digestible, familiar stereotypes and told through the lens of a white person. The author identified as a white woman before embracing her Latinx grandparent. But the dubious ethics of her identity aside, it took a white woman, a white Latina if we are being generous, to translate our experience from English to whiteness. I cannot think of any other book with undocumented immigrants as the protagonists that became one of the bestselling novels for an entire year. Certainly none that were written by undocumented or formerly undocumented immigrants. As long as society continues to validate our humanity through the eyes of white people, publishers, marketers, and TV execs will continue to place the success of our work in the hands of a white audience.

I joined the many Latinx writers who spoke out about *American Dirt*, the most scathing and powerful of reviews written by Myriam Gurba. The book had many issues within its pages—the stereotypes, the flat characters—but the way the book was *made* into a success pointed to much larger structural problems in publishing, and in turn those problems pointed to even bigger societal truths. The book allowed white people to observe fictional, respectable, whitewashed characters from a safe distance instead of the real people who immigrate to America. People who are imperfect. People who aren't a sad story, or a thrilling one, or always extraordinary. People who are just people.

I was invited to speak on *Oprah's Book Club* on Apple TV+ about the book and about the broken state of the publishing industry. I joined two other Latinx authors, my friend Reyna Grande and Esther Cepeda; the author of *American Dirt*; and Oprah. I didn't hold my tongue. Toward the end of the first segment, I turned to the author and asked her, "Who did you write this book for?" In the author's note of her book, she wrote that she had "the capacity to be a bridge," and I wanted to know who she imagined would be walking across it.

"You're saying you wanted to use your book to change people's minds," I said.

The author, visibly uncomfortable, said, "Of course."

I pressed her. "So whose minds?"

She struggled to come up with an answer. "The readers' minds," she replied. "I don't have a conglomerate reader. I wrote the book because I hoped it would move people."

And there I had my answer. In the author's note, she had also written that she wanted to help readers see immigrants as fellow human beings. If her desire was to change the minds of those who think of us as "an invading mob of resource-draining criminals" or "a faceless brown mass," as she wrote, and to bring them across the bridge, then she couldn't possibly have centered us in her book. We don't think of ourselves as faceless or as voiceless. We have powerful things to say.

Her story was written with a white reader in mind, or at least a reader who had not experienced what her characters had—a perfectly set-up obstacle course meant to reflect a perilous immigration journey. It is no wonder that the book had to be crafted in such an apolitical way. But we cannot divorce the political from the human condition of immigrants. Policy issues are a direct consequence of our moral and humanitarian shortcomings. Deciding to be silent on matters of policy is in itself a political stance.

TV executives want to tell our stories, but they don't want to offend a white audience and therefore make immigrants caricatures that can make them cry, or laugh. We can be Chola #1 or Maid #5, but rarely a leading lady. And when we are a main character, she must be the whitest possible version.

I love HGTV shows. They are my wine and chocolate. I particularly like the remodeling shows. There is something so satisfying about seeing beauty blossom where once there was nothing but ugliness. Those transformations are made possible by mostly Latino men. You can catch a glimpse of their hands as they put in new floors, or see the back of their baseball hats as they install a backsplash in the kitchen. But you never hear them speak. It bothers me that the camera can't even show their full faces or their whole bodies; we see only their labor. That's what we are to America, fragments.

Newspapers write only about the most moving narratives, or the most salacious. My own story has been used to propel the myth of a perfect immigrant. I tell reporters and documentary directors the nuances of my life—how it wasn't all roses. I emphasize the thorns. But when I see their finished work, it's like the Rose Day Parade. I struggle with how my life is used as inspiration for us, but also as a form of pandering to white people. But my intentions with my own work, with my own words, is clear.

During the Apple TV+ special, I shared a story about Georgia Clark, a teacher in Texas who was fired after she sent a series of tweets to Trump (when he still had an account), one of which read, "I really do need a contact here in Fort Worth who should be actively investigating and removing the illegals that are in the public school system." Eighteen years ago, I was one of those "illegals" at a public high school in Texas. Luckily, my teacher, Mr. Gnospelius, didn't want me deported; instead he wanted me to go to college.

I told the audience that I am less interested in writing with Georgia Clark as my reader and more concerned with using my writing to help her students feel seen, loved, and understood. I might never be able to change Georgia Clark's mind on why she is wrong about her students, many of whom are actually U.S. citizens, born in America with brown skin. But I can keep writing stories that are relevant to her students. Stories that make sense to them. English that tells these young people, who may be undocumented or have parents who are undocumented, or who are American-born Latinos, or who are people of color, that they don't have to shrink themselves to keep others at ease.

My hope is that my stories will help them take up space in their classrooms, in their neighborhoods, and in this country. I want my community not to have to explain; I want us to simply to be able to exist. We cannot make ourselves or allow others to make us small so we can fit in the minds and hearts of white people. America might never love us back, so we must love ourselves.

After the show taped, I stopped by the greenroom to pick up my suitcase before I headed to the airport. Oprah asked if I had said everything I wanted to say. She said she could tell that I "especially" had a lot to share. I didn't get to say everything I wanted, but when I walked off the stage, I felt proud of how I showed up for my community. If I am going to tell stories, it's not going to be to get white people to see me as human. It's going to be to stand up for us. It's going to be to say, I see you, and I love you.

We Are Our Own Savior

> *I've got lots of heroes in me. Because I am Cesar Chavez, and I am Céspedes of the Mets, even though he's always injured. And I am Menudo. And I am Sonia Sotomayor. And I am definitely not Ted Cruz . . . As one of my fellow classmates once said to me, "You're the king of nothing." But if the Mayans invented the concept of zero . . . then nothing is not nothing. And if they can make something out of nothing . . . then my hero is . . . . My . . . hero . . . is . . . me.*
>
> —JOHN LEGUIZAMO, *Latin History for Morons*

During the Covid-19 pandemic, I joined a Zoom event that celebrated a distinguished panel of women activists, entrepreneurs, scientists, and artists. During the event, a high-profile art dealer was asked about the role of art during pandemics. She spoke about the Renaissance coming out of the Black Death, the pandemic that killed hundreds of millions of people in Asia, North Africa, and Europe between 1346 and 1353. The comment felt insensitive, given that thousands of people were burying loved ones, and hundreds of thousands more people remained sick from the coronavirus, as if beautiful art somehow made their suffering worth it. To make matters worse, she proceeded to say that during the 1400s, Michelangelo, Leonardo, Raphael, and other artists "we know by [their] first name" were creating masterpieces while America had not even been discovered.

The notion that Europeans were superior in every way, biologically and culturally, is a gross lie that white people have believed, and sadly some of us have as well, for far too long. We are a people rich in history, art, and innovation. Never forget that by the time the colonizers came to the Americas we had already built pyramids so magnificent that, to this day, some believe they must have been built by aliens. We had created chocolate. We had made advanced mathematical discoveries. We had studied the stars in the constellations that light the sky. Since before history was recorded, Indigenous people created art, made babies, sang, fought epic battles, lived. The story of our indigenous ancestors doesn't begin or end with colonization.

The land of native people in the Americas was stolen, our art destroyed, our customs taken from us. Assimilation forced upon our children. Hundreds of years later, we are still subjected to bursts of superiority. Colonizers stole from us then, and people today want to continue to take our heritage, making us believe that we don't have a history so they can continue to trick us into assimilation, so they can hold the power.

I sat uncomfortably trying not to let my face show the

anger building in my chest. I had thought I was in a safe space. I wasn't a guest on Fox News. This panel was supposed to be a celebration of women who'd broken barriers, who had stood up for their communities, who are extraordinary. The panel was "diverse." Of the nine women, five of us were women of color. But as one of my fellow panelists later told me, "It's a classic issue of forgetting the inclusivity part of diversity and inclusion." I once heard someone say that diversity is being invited to the dance and inclusion is being asked to dance. Still, it is always assumed that the inviting, the asking, is done by white people. I am tired of this language that still centers our value and worth around whiteness. Diversity, inclusion, and equity are insufficient to describe justice.

In 2020, here was a "progressive" white woman making comments about the "discovery" of America. Her words suggested those already on the American continent were simply waiting around to be found and saved. I was furious. Her comment was strongly indicative of the deep-seated feeling of superiority so many white Americans, even some progressive ones, still maintain as truth.

The next time I was asked a question, I took the opportunity to speak up. "I want to comment on something that was said earlier about America being discovered while Europe was having the Renaissance," I said into my computer. "That's a very common misconception that America was discovered. We've always been here . . . the unfortunate reality is that the beautiful, amazing pieces of artwork that were created by Native people in America sadly were destroyed by colonizers. We don't have those masterpieces that we would have if they had been left untouched."

The most enraging part about the suggestion that Europeans have a greater heritage than ours is that the reason so much of our art and so many of our traditions and customs have vanished is because Europeans stole it from us. And so much of what is left sits in museums across Europe and the United States or in the private collections of rich people. The looting of our heritage still continues. In 2013, the Mexican government demanded that Sotheby's halt the auction of dozens of pre-Columbian national historical artifacts. The sculptures, ceramics, and textiles belong to the Mexican people, not in the hands of collectors. The sale went ahead. In 2019, the Aztec goddess of running water and patron of childbirth was sold for €377,000 at another contested auction. The Guatemalan government has tried to stop ten different auctions since 2010, yet all of them have proceeded, though it did get Sotheby's to withdraw one piece from a 2013 auction. As the comedian Sam Jay said after visiting the British Museum in London, "White people stole all this shit. Stole so much shit. All this shit is stolen. . . . The audacity . . . [to] charge [us] $20 to see it. [Our] own shit."[1]

After my comments during the panel, I texted a friend: "why is it so hard to speak up! I am glad I said something but now I am shaking."

Her response was perfect: "Because we are conditioned to find it hard. If we didn't, imagine all the things the privileged would be forced to hear." It is time for the privileged to hear the truth. It is time to stamp out every false belief, to breathe truth into history, to recognize that we carry with us thousands of years of survival.

These lies creep into and live comfortably in the minds of even those who claim to love and respect us. A couple of years ago, I had dinner with a group of friends at a fancy sushi restaurant in New York City. We sat in a private room eating sashimi, drinking sake, and having a *light* conversation about politics. Everyone seated at the table was progressive. My French friend perhaps more so—socialism is not a scary monster to him. We've had plenty of conversations over the years that made me trust him as an ally.

The talk turned to the topic of immigration, he also being an immigrant to the United States. I spoke of the push and pull of immigration, how the United States creates conditions in Latin America that force people to migrate north.

I forget what led to his next statement, but my brain froze upon hearing it. "Where would you be if we hadn't colonized you?" It wasn't the first time a well-meaning white friend made an offhanded racist remark. Nevertheless, I was dumbfounded that my friend believed that Indigenous people needed saving.

The French weren't very successful at colonizing Mexico, not even with the help of the United States. The Cinco de Mayo holiday that white Americans love to celebrate commemorates the Battle of Puebla, in which an outnumbered Mexican army of mostly Indigenous fighters defeated the French. A battle that Mexicans in California at that time viewed as a win against slavery because of Napoleon III's interest in aiding the Confederacy.[2] For many years after, Californios held parades dressed in Civil War uniforms and celebrated the Battle of Puebla as part of the abolition struggle. But I knew he meant in general, where would *we*, Mexicans, Latinos, be if *they*, Europeans, white people, hadn't come to our rescue?

I know one thing: we didn't need to be saved.

My heart breaks when I see a Brown person question our own value in the same way that woman on the panel or my French friend did. But isn't that why we assimilate, after all, because, ultimately, we believe white is better, an easier form of existing in the world?

I was having a conversation with a relative about the Mexican-American War, and he said, "But think about it. It's better that California and Texas became part of the United States. Otherwise we'd be in the condition that Mexico is in." That's the toxicity of assimilation, constantly making us question our value, our worth, our abilities. The disparity in economic development between the United States, Mexico, and Latin America has nothing to do with racial superiority or the idea that the American founders were smarter or better at establishing a nation. The inequity has been building from the very start of our colonization. The relationship between Spanish colonizers and Indigenous people in Mexico was as violent as the relationship between the British and the Native people in the United States. But there was one key difference. The Pilgrims that came over on the *Mayflower* didn't come seeking to take back the riches they found. They came with the intention to develop and stay on the land they stole. They invested in their own growth. They waged an intentional genocide and placed the survivors out of sight on reservations, where Native people today continue to feel the consequences caused by white settlers.

The riches of Latin America, the gold, silver, and natural resources, made it a target for colonization, but the Spanish didn't come to grow anything. Instead they came to take, to exploit, to mine our wealth and leave us hollow and empty. No one knows where Latin America would be if it weren't for "the genocide, the cruelty, the abuse, and the exploitation exerted upon the people of Latin America," as Isabel Allende writes.[3] Perhaps without the disease and violence Europeans brought, we would have continued to evolve our thriving civilizations free of colonization and white supremacy. I like to imagine that we'd be more powerful than the United States—not because we developed the same oppressive systems America did, but because we'd been spared of their influence.

Instead, we were left to build on the ashes the Spanish discarded, with a neighbor to the north that would meddle in Latin American affairs for centuries to come. The United States didn't stop with the colonization of Mexico. In 1855, William Walker invaded Nicaragua with the support of the U.S. government. Walker declared himself president of Nicaragua, El Salvador, and Honduras. He brought back slavery in the places he occupied. The United States practically stole Colombian land to create Panama so they could move between two oceans. From 1915 to 1934, the United States occupied Haiti. They continued to manipulate Mexico through intervening during the Mexican Revolution, with the building of maquiladoras in Juárez that enrich white men and make Mexicans the enemy, as well as currently detaining tens of thousands of asylum seekers in migrant camps along the Mexico-U.S. border. The United States became the colonizer of the Americas long after we'd won our freedom from European imperialism. America has always placed its own interests—rather than the tenet of freedom for all—above all else.

From sugar to coffee to rubber, Latin America has provided all the key ingredients for the "first world" countries to succeed. It is the consumption of our materials that has made the United States a rich country.

Colonization benefited only the colonizer and the crowns they served. Their success was not earned but stolen:

native lands, Black people they enslaved, Indigenous women they forcefully took as wives. Their success is the result of our oppression.

That people of color have managed to find a way to thrive despite all of this is a testament to the resilience and power that have been passed down from our ancestors and still flow through our veins. Imagine for one moment how powerful we are that after centuries of efforts to erase us, we are here in bright and living colors! And still after centuries of surviving and even thriving, despite continued U.S. and European intervention in Latin America for their own purposes and benefit, white people still believe we needed their saving. They still demand we assimilate to their culture because they believe it superior. They still maintain, as President William Howard Taft declared in 1912, that "by virtue of [their] superiority of race," they were morally entitled "to the whole hemisphere," to our bodies, and to our fate. It is this belief that continues to exhaust Latin America, to rob the workers of their lungs, and keep us, Latinos, in America as unequal in our own country.

With rumbling stomachs, we cross deserts and oceans. We continue to make space in a land that is ours, in spite of a system that doesn't want us. Many argue that the United States doesn't owe anything to the world, and therefore we shouldn't have to take in immigrants and refugees. In fact, this country owes a great debt to the poor and hungry people of the world on whom its success has been built.

It's not an easy task to unburden ourselves from all the lies we learned growing up, from the idea that we needed to shed our uniqueness in order to be worthy of the world around us. It's time we break free from the muzzles that keep us quiet for the sake of keeping others comfortable in their lies and power. We have to drop some knowledge so they don't continue to take from us. Today, I am armed with knowledge that allows me to stand in my truth, to push back, and to call out deceitful information that keeps the illusion of white superiority alive.

It is time to reclaim everything that is ours. There are so many things we call "white people shit," like hiking, camping, and visiting national parks and forests. Partly, some of those activities prove too expensive for many people in our community. Who has time to go visit a national park in the middle of nowhere when there is food to put on the table? But I no longer call it "white people shit," because it is in fact ours. Many of the national parks in the Western United States exist on land that was Mexican before it was American, and Native American before and after it was Mexican. It is ours to enjoy, to maintain, and to pass on to generations after us. The land, the mountains, the trees whose roots are centuries old are part of the stories of our ancestors who roamed those lands. All that beauty has survived to remind us of the strength that lives in us.

·7·

Last Words

We have to create new spaces, new systems, new rules that are built on truth and justice for all. We have the luxury of learning from the mistakes of the past reminding ourselves of what's already been done on our behalf.

Movements of the past have failed to understand the intersectionality of our struggles. In 1957, Felix Tijerina, president of League of United Latin American Citizens (LULA) from 1956 to 1960, famously said, "Let the Negro fight his own battles. His problems are not mine. I don't want to ally with him." But there was also Reies Lopez Tijerina, who is often confused with Felix; he did know how our fights, while unique, were stronger together. He led the Latino coalition for the Poor People's March on Washington. He organized with Black Panther leader Bobby Seale. He spoke at the Free Huey rally in 1968 after Black Panther co-founder Huey P. Newton was arrested in October

1967. The United Farm Workers Organizing Committee joined hands with Martin Luther King Jr., understanding that there was power in impoverished people of all colors coming together. They wrote, "we have a debt to Dr. King, a debt larger than to any living man."

While in prison, Huey Newton recorded a message of support for Los Siete de la Raza, a group of seven young Latinos from the Mission District of San Francisco who were accused of murdering a cop (the cop was shot with his partner's gun) in 1969. (Six of Los Siete de la Raza were ultimately acquitted, the seventh was never taken into custody.) His words remind me of how we must show up for each other. "I want you to know that . . . the Black Community is behind you in your struggle 100 percent. And it is our intention to help you in everything possible until [you] are set free." He went on to urge the young men to maintain a good spirit because "it is necessary to overcome the obstacles and the oppression that confronts us." He ended his message with "Black Power to Black People. Brown Power to Brown People. Power to all the Oppressed People of the World."[1]

It's not only the Black-Brown fractures, but the ones we've created between those born on this side and those born on the other. Cesar Chavez, probably the best-known Latino activist, was notoriously against undocumented workers because he viewed them as strikebreakers in his fight for fair treatment of farmworkers. In a letter to the editor of the *San Francisco Examiner*, Chavez wrote: "If there were no illegals being used to break our strikes, we could win those strikes overnight and then be in a position to improve the living and working conditions of all farm workers." I celebrate Cesar Chavez for his efforts to bring dignity to farmworkers. None of us are without flaw. Still, others understood how resisting together was the real answer. In 1972, Chicano students rejected the idea that their undocumented brethren were responsible for their pain; instead they viewed them as part of their struggle. A young activist wrote in the Los Angeles Chicano newspaper *Regeneración*: "It is claimed that illegals cause high unemployment of residents; that they oppose the formation of unions; that they drain residents' incomes by adding to welfare costs . . . These claims are fake . . . [they] do not create unemployment of Chicanos, employers desiring to pay the lowest possible wages do." These young activists understood that the answer to equality lived with all of us.

My wish is that more people will learn about the beautiful, authentic, and respectful ways in which we have come together. We have to heal the wounds that for many are still bleeding. Yes, Latinos have harbored racist ideas toward African Americans and Black Latinos. Miya Ponsetto, a white Puerto Rican woman, was famously caught on video tackling a Black teenager after accusing him of stealing her phone. African Americans have held anti-immigrant sentiments. A video in the summer of 2020 showed Latino workers leaving a construction site, and a group of Black protesters yelling "go back to where you came from," and carrying signs that read: "Stop stealing our jobs." Asian and Black communities have had rifts, some of which were still seen in 2021, when a slew of violent crimes against elderly Asians were caught on camera. We have to be honest about the harm we do to one another. If we are to dismantle white supremacy, we have to recognize the role we are playing to advance it.

Having these conversations is difficult, and we likely won't get it right the first time. But we cannot let fear of perfection keep us from making progress. Grace has to be a big part of it. We have to give room to one another to make mistakes and move forward. I am full of hope that together we can change the entire world.

The intersectional justice movement of today is showing us how to do it. We're still not perfect, but the 2020 election was a glorious example of how multiracial coalitions can deliver wins for all people. Georgia turned blue for the first time in nearly thirty years thanks to the leadership of Black women. In Arizona, Latinos of all backgrounds, and Indigenous coalitions, helped deliver a democratic win by turning the state blue for the first time since the election of Bill Clinton in 1996. Together—Indigenous,

African American, Latino, and Asian communities—we are creating change.

Today, immigrant rights organizers know that immigration is not only a Latino issue. The fastest-growing immigrant group is Asians. Black immigrants are deported at much higher rates than others, so immigration is also a racial justice issue. Criminal justice reform activists understand the intersections of police and immigration enforcement. The two systems are rotten apples from the same tree. An interaction with racist police can lead to deportation. As the federal government moves away from for-profit prisons, those companies have turned their attention to immigrant detention camps, and so the fight continues. Feminists know that there can be no reproductive rights without racial justice and without an inclusive gender lens. Justice is all interconnected.

For me, writing, and putting pen to paper on this book in particular, has been a liberating journey. I more deeply understand that our solutions are in us, not in the false promise of assimilation. I don't want an America that stays true to America, I want an America that challenges the status quo. One that revises its story to fully tell our shared history, facing the ugliness of the past, admitting the sins of our founding, and creating a truer democracy. It starts with us. Belonging is about acceptance, and, for us, that means accepting our power.

"We the People of the United States" must include

all the people who have made America. From the Native people of this land, to the Mexicans who've been here for centuries, to the Black person whose ancestors' bondage was this country's freedom, to the Chinese laborer who built the railroads—each of us is the people.

"In order to form a more perfect Union, establish Justice," we must actually seek justice. Assimilation, diversity, inclusion—this is not justice. Representation is justice. Equality is justice. Intersection is justice. Freedom is justice.

Let's get off the track. Let's go in search of freedom.

Postscript

There are moments in life that mark a before and after. August 3, 2019, was a day like that for me. What happened in El Paso broke me. I saw it so clearly: no matter what we do, some people will never see us as American. They will view us as a threat. But I started thinking, *What are they so afraid of—our beauty, our passion, our laughter?*

As the days passed and the news coverage carried on, the nation forgot to remember El Paso. On the one-year anniversary of the terrorist attack carried out in the name of whiteness, not a single major newspaper ran a front-page story. I cannot imagine any other tragedy being forgotten so quickly. Twenty-three people, mostly Americans, had been killed on August 3, 2019, and a year later, the country had moved on.

Our community had not. I will never forget. To honor the victims of El Paso, to honor the beauty for which they were killed, I wrote about the invasion that laughs and sings and dances: our beautiful people. I want to share that beauty with you.

An Invasion Dances

For El Paso and Mexicanos.

° ° °

What kind of invasion laughs so joyfully
It fills our bellies like a barril de olla
& our eyes water with tears that twirl

° ° °

What kind of invasion is so colorful
is shaped in red, purple, yellow flowers made of paper
Like the dresses of folklórico
Like the piñatas we break at the bautizo, the tres años,
and every year in between and after
A deep mole red

° ° °

What kind of invasion plays the guitar
the violin in a charro suit
and it makes you get up and dance
And cry sometimes too
Plays banda at the wedding

° ° °

What kind of invasion invents chocolate
Oh yeah, we did that

We studied the stars in the constellations that light the sky
Painted masterpieces
Became masterpieces

• • •

An invasion of anchor babies?
Anchors attached to the bed of this land
With roots connecting us to magueys of Oaxaca
to the quiet waves of Veracruz
to the rolling hills of Taxco
to the purple prickly nopales of El Paso
And all the way to Montana

• • •

What kind of invasion fills rooms with laughter
and dances
and climbs mountains and defies the desert
and tends the ground with care and love

• • •

Our spirit can't be shattered by a bullet.
So we dance, and we laugh, and we breathe, and we stay.
We stay, stay, stay.

Acknowledgments

Gracias a la vida because I was born Mexican. Mamá y papá, soy quien soy because you taught me how to be. Always all the love to mi tío Mike, who taught me to love books, to have a curiosity for life. To Nay, Aris, y Julio, los quiero mucho. Gracias por ser mis hermanos. Julio, thank you, little brother, for always answering my calls and centering me. To the ancestors, your survival is my survival. To all the revisionist historians, the Chicano authors, the Latino leaders, your work changed my life. It filled the cracks left by the force of assimilation. It healed me.

This book would not be possible without Lisa Leshne, my literary agent and friend, who never stopped believing in this book, or in me. Your tenacity to get it published kept me energized even as we revised our proposal a thousand and one times. I am forever grateful for your friendship and perfect agent skills.

There aren't enough flowers to give to Bryn Clark, my editor. You saw what this book could be and shepherded it into existence. Writing it has been one of the most difficult tasks of my life, and your patience, pep talks, and deep belief that people needed to read what I wrote gave me the confidence that I could, that I would, write a powerful book. The entire editorial team at Flatiron was amazing, but a very special thank you to Caroline Bleeke, for your guidance while we all missed Bryn. I'll always remember what you said to me about drafts requiring ugly scaffolding, but eventually a beautiful building emerges. Wrapping my mind around how to organize this book was headache inducing, and your vision was the remedy I needed. To Ruben Reyes, thank you for stepping up each time.

To the entire publicity, marketing, and sales team, and especially Nancy Trypuc, Amelia Possanza, Jordan Forney, and Malati Chavali, yours is the very difficult job of getting people to buy this book. You've made me feel like mine is the only title you are working on. Thank you for everything you have done and are doing to get my writing into the hands of actual, real people. To Megan Lynch, Flatiron's publisher, I am deeply grateful for your personal involvement in this book and commitment to my work. Thank you.

Reyna Grande, my friend, mentor, hermana, thank you for reading the earliest manuscript and giving me notes even as you wrote your latest novel. I'll always thank life for bringing us together from Guerrero to California where our friendship blossomed. To Maeve Higgins, Xelena González, Jean Guerrero, and Nydia Simone, thank you for your invaluable guidance. To José Olivarez, amigo, thank you for your notes, kindness, and poetry. You are a real homie.

On days when I couldn't see through the haze of life, Carlos Hernandez and Jazmin Morales, my dearest friends, you provided cocktails and, most importantly, laughter, love, and support, the kind that only comes from family. To Justin, thank you for letting me use your apartment as a writing alcove. It was just the place I needed when lockdown took away coffee shops.

I wrote this book during one of the hardest moments in human history. Writing during a global pandemic could have broken me, but you, my best friend, my life partner, mi licenciado, my husband, Fernando, you are a fountain of love, laughter, and wisdom. I love you more than words could describe. You have shown me what love is. Contigo vamos por todo. Te amo.

Y Dios, most of all, you are the reason why.

Notes

Introduction

[1] Lee and Low Books, Laura M. Jiménez, and Betsy Beckert, "Where is the diversity in publishing? The 2019 Diversity Baseline Survey Results," *Lee & Low Books* (blog), January 28, 2020, https://blog.leeandlow.com/2020/01/28/2019diversitybaselinesurvey/.

[2] Denise Lu, Jon Huang, Ashwin Seshagiri, Haeyoun Park, and Troy Griggs, "Faces of Power: 80% Are White, Even as U.S. Becomes More Diverse," *The New York Times*, September 9, 2020, https://www.nytimes.com/interactive/2020/09/09/us/powerful-people-race-us.html.

[3] "Race/ethnicity of college faculty," National Center for Education Statistics, accessed May 24, 2020, https://nces.ed.gov/FastFacts/display.asp?id=6; "Teacher characteristics and trends," National Center for Education Statistics, accessed May 24, 2020, https://nces.ed.gov/FastFacts/display.asp?id=28.

[4] William H. Frey, "The US will become 'minority white' in 2045, Census projects," *Brookings*, March 14, 2018, https://www.brookings.edu/blog/the-avenue/2018/03/14/the-us-will-become-minority-white-in-2045-census-projects/.

1. The Lie of Whiteness

[1] Aaron O'Neill, "Languages in Mexico 2005," Statista, https://www.statista.com/statistics/275440/languages-in-mexico/.

[2] David M. Traboulay, *Columbus and Las Casas: The Conquest and Christianization of America, 1492–1566* (Lanham, MD: University Press of America, 1994), 58.

[3] David Agren,"'We exist. We're here': Afro-Mexicans make the census after long struggle for recognition," *The Guardian*, March 19, 2020, https://www.theguardian.com/world/2020/mar/19/afro-mexicans-census-history-identity.

[4] Ellwood P. Cubberley, *Changing Conceptions of Education* (Boston, MA: Houghton Mifflin Co., 1909).

[5] Miranda E. Wilkerson and Joseph Salmons, "'GOOD Old Immigrants of Yesteryear,' Who Didn't Learn English: Germans in Wisconsin," *American Speech* 83, no. 3 (2008): 259–83. https://doi.org/10.1215/00031283-2008-020.

[6] David Roediger, *Working Toward Whiteness: How America's Immigrants Became White: The Strange Journey from Ellis Island to the Suburbs* (New York: Basic Books, 2005), 3.

[7] Noel Ignatiev, *How the Irish Became White* (New York: Routledge, 1995), 124.

[8] Ann Coulter, *Adios, America: The Left's Plan to Turn Our Country into a Third World Hellhole* (Washington, D.C.: Regnery Publishing, 2015), 27.

[9] Ben Collins, "Investigators 'Reasonably Confident' Texas Suspect Left Anti-Immigrant Screed, Tipped Off Before Attack," *NBC News*, August 3, 2019, https://www.nbcnews.com/news/us-news/investigators-reasonably-confident-texas-suspect-left-anti-immigrant-screed-tipped-n1039031; "Federal Grand Jury in El Paso Returns Superseding Indictment against Patrick Crusius," United States Department of Justice, July 9, 2020, https://www.justice.gov/usao-wdtx/pr/federal-grand-jury-el-paso-returns-superseding-indictment-against-patrick-crusius.

[10] Peter Brimelow, *Alien Nation: Common Sense about America's Immigration Disaster* (New York: Random House, 1995).

[11] "Hispanic Heritage Month 2020," U.S. Census Bureau, accessed May 27, 2021, https://www.census.gov/newsroom/facts-for-features/2020/hispanic-heritage-month.html; Mark H. López, Jens M. Krogstad, and Antonio Flores, "Key facts about young Latinos, one of the nation's fastest-growing populations," Pew Research Center, September 13, 2018, https://www.pewresearch.org/fact-tank/2018/09/13/key-facts-about-young-latinos/#:~:text=born.,Latinos%20ages%2036%20or%20older.

[12] Julia Carrie Wong, "Trump Referred to Immigrant 'Invasion' in 2,000 Facebook Ads, Analysis Reveals," *The Guardian*, August 5, 2019.

[13] John Fritze, "Trump Used Words Like 'Invasion' and 'Killer' to Discuss Immigrants at Rallies 500 Times: USA Today Analysis," *USA Today*, August 21, 2019.

[14] Adrian Carrasquillo, "This Is What Latinos Think Everyone Got Wrong About El Paso," *Politico Magazine*, August 10, 2019.

[15] Martha Menchaca, *Recovering History, Constructing Race: The Indian, Black, and White Roots of Mexican Americans* (Austin: University of Texas Press, 2002).

[16] Paul Ortiz, *An African American and Latinx History of the United States* (Boston: Beacon Press, 2018).

[17] Laura E. Gómez, *Manifest Destinies: The Making of the Mexican American Race*, 2nd ed. (New York: New York University Press, 2018), 63.

[18] Gómez, *Manifest Destinies*, 18.

[19] Gómez, *Manifest Destinies*, 174.

[20] Gómez, *Manifest Destinies*, xvii.

[21] James C. Ho, "Defining 'American': Birthright Citizenship and the Original Understanding of the 14th Amendment," *The Green Bag* 9, no. 4 (2006). https://www.gibsondunn.com/wp-content/uploads/documents/publications/Ho-DefiningAmerican.pdf.

[22] Gómez, *Manifest Destinies*, 148.

[23] Matt Stevens, "9-Year-Old Girl Was Detained at Border for 30 Hours Despite Being a U.S. Citizen," *The New York Times*, March 22, 2019.

[24] U.S. Government Accountability Office, "Immigration Enforcement: Actions Needed to Better Handle, Identify, and Track Cases Involving Veterans," GAO-19-416, June 2019, https://www.gao.gov/assets/gao-19-416.pdf.

[25] Aprile D. Benner et al., "Racial/Ethnic Discrimination and Well-Being During Adolescence: A Meta-Analytic Review," *American Psychologist* 73, no. 7 (2018): 855–83. http://dx.doi.org/10.1037/amp0000204.

2. The Lie of English

[1] Karla Cornejo Villavicencio, *The Undocumented Americans* (New York: One World, 2020), 18.

[2] Kristi L. Bowman, "The New Face of School Desegregation," *Duke Law Journal* 50, no. 6 (2001): 1751–808. Accessed June 28, 2021. doi:10.2307/1373047.

[3] Bowman, "The New Face of School Desegregation."

[4] "Status Dropout Rates," National Center for Education Statistics, last updated May 2021, https://nces.ed.gov/programs/coe/indicator/coj.

[5] "Racial and Ethnic Composition of the Child Population," Child Trends, 2018, accessed May 2, 2020, https://www.childtrends.org/indicators/racial-and-ethnic-composition-of-the-child-population.

[6] Kristin Lam and Erin Richards, "More US Schools Teach in English and Spanish, but Not Enough to Help Latino Kids," *USA Today*, January 6, 2020, https://www.usatoday.com/in-depth/news/education/2020/01/06/english-language-learners-benefit-from-dual-language-immersion-bilingual-education/4058632002/.

[7] Reyna Grande, "I Lost My Mother Tongue—and Almost My Mom," CNN, February 28, 2019, https://www.cnn.com/2019/02/28/opinions/bilingualism-spanish-english-power-of-language-grande/index.html.

[8] Nicole Acevedo, "White Customer at Mexican Restaurant Swears at Spanish-Speaking Manager," NBC News, February 19, 2019, https://www.nbcnews.com/news/latino/white-customer-mexican-restaurant-swears-spanish-speaking-manager-n973191.

[9] Allyson Waller, "U.S. Border Agency Settles with 2 Americans Detained for Speaking Spanish," *The New York Times,* November 26, 2020, https://www.nytimes.com/2020/11/26/us/montana-spanish-border-patrol.html.

[10] Antonia Hernández, "Chicanas and the Issue of Involuntary Sterilization: Reforms Needed to Protect Informed Consent," *Chicano Law Review* 3, no. 3 (1976): 3–37. https://escholarship.org/content/qt35v8r48h/qt35v8r48h.pdf.

[11] Marcela Valdes, "When Doctors Took 'Family Planning' Into Their Own Hands," *The New York Times*, February 1, 2016, https://www.nytimes.com/2016/02/01/magazine/when-doctors-took-family-planning-into-their-own-hands.html.

[12] Alexandra M. Stern, *Eugenic Nation: Faults and Frontiers of Better Breeding in Modern America*, 2nd ed. (Oakland: University of California Press, 2015), 231. Kindle.

[13] Stern, *Eugenic Nation*, 231.

[14] Brittny Mejia, "'You Need to Speak English': Encounters in Viral Videos Show Spanish Is Still Polarizing in the U.S.," *Los Angeles Times*, May 28, 2018, https://www.latimes.com/local/california/la-me-ln-speak-english-20180528-story.html.

[15] Tina Vásquez, "The National Lawyers Guild's Former First 'Latina' President Is a White Woman," *Prism,* January 7, 2021, https://prismreports

.org/2021/01/07/the-national-lawyers-guilds-outgoing-latina-president-is-a-white-woman/.

[16] Nestor Gomez, "Movie Night," NPR *Moth Radio Hour*, https://themoth.org/storytellers/nestor-gomez.

[17] Perales7676, "Edcouch-Elsa Walkout school boycott 1968 CBS Broadcast Walter Cronkite," Youtube video, https://www.youtube.com/watch?v=xU-zQBvgn-k.

3. The Lie of Success

[1] Martin Gilens, "How the Poor Became Black: The Racialization of American Poverty in the Mass Media," in *Race and the Politics of Welfare Reform*, eds. Sanford F. Schram, Joe Soss, and Richard C. Fording (Ann Arbor: University of Michigan Press, 2003), 101–30.

[2] Viviana López Green and Samantha Vargas Poppe, "Toward a More Perfect Union: Understanding Systemic Racism and Resulting Inequity in Latino Communities," UnidosUS, April 2021, http://publications.nclr.org/handle/123456789/2128.

[3] Ann Coulter, *Adios, America: The Left's Plan to Turn Our Country into a Third World Hellhole* (Washington, D.C.: Regnery Publishing, 2015).

[4] Patricia Escárcega, "'Mexican Food Always Wins': José R. Ralat on His New Book 'American Tacos,'" *Los Angeles Times,* April 21, 2020, https://www.latimes.com/food/story/2020-04-21/interview-with-taco-editor-jose-ralat-book-american-tacos?_amp=true&__twitter_impression=true.

[5] Roy Germano, "Unauthorized Immigrants Paid $100 Billion Into Social Security Over Last Decade," *Vice News*, August 4, 2014, https://www.vice.com/en/article/zm5k8j/unauthorized-immigrants-paid-100-billion-into-social-security-over-last-decade.

[6] Zaiour, Giovanni Peri and Reem. "Citizenship for Undocumented Immigrants Would Boost U.S. Economic Growth." Center for American Progress. Accessed July 8, 2021. https://www.americanprogress.org/issues/immigration/reports/2021/06/14/500433/citizenship-undocumented-immigrants-boost-u-s-economic-growth/.

[7] Coulter, *Adios America,* 86.

[8] Jessica Semega, Melissa Kollar, John Creamer, and Abinash Mohanty, "Income and Poverty in the United States: 2018," U.S. Census Bureau report P60-266, September 10, 2019, https://www.census.gov/library/publications/2019/demo/p60-266.html.

[9] Rachel Siegel, "Wealth Gaps Between Black and White Families Persisted Even a the Height of the Economic Expansion," *The Washington Post*, September 28, 2020, https://www.washingtonpost.com/business/2020/09/28/wealth-gap-fed/.

[10] Noel Ignatiev, *How the Irish Became White* (New York: Routledge, 1995), 129.

[11] Zaragosa Vargas, *Crucible of Struggle: A History of Mexican Americans from Colonial Times to the Present Era* (New York: Oxford University Press, 2010).

[12] Louis Menand, "The Changing Meaning of Affirmative Action: The Past and the Future of a Long-Embattled Policy," *The New Yorker*, January 13, 2020, https://www.newyorker.com/magazine/2020/01/20/have-we-outgrown-the-need-for-affirmative-action.

[13] Latina Lista, "Without Intervention, Latino Millennials on Same Path as Parents Towards Financial Insecurity," The Smart News Source, August 27, 2014, http://latinalista.com/culture-2/without-intervention-latino-millennials-path-parents-towards-financial-insecurity#8230.

[14] "What Percentage of Americans Own Stock?," USA Facts, last modified March 9, 2021, https://usafacts.org/articles/what-percentage-of-americans-own-stock/; Carmen Reinicke, "The Pandemic Has Made the Racial Retirement Gap Worse. Here's How Individuals Can Close It," NBC News, November 15, 2020, https://www.nbcnews.com/news/nbcblk/pandemic-has-made-racial-retirement-gap-worse-here-s-how-n1247771.

4. Reclaiming Our History

[1] Eduardo Galeano, *Open Veins of Latin America: Five Centuries of the Pillage of a Continent, 25th Anniversary Edition* (New York: Monthly Review Press, 1997), 71.

[2] Paul Ortiz, *An African American and Latinx History of the United States* (Boston: Beacon Press, 2018), 7.

[3] Dr. Darnell Hunt, Dr. Ana-Christina Ramón, and Michael Tran, *Hollywood Diversity Report, Old Story, New Beginning,* UCLA College Social Sciences, accessed March 29, 2020, https://socialsciences.ucla.edu/hollywood-diversity-report-2019/.

[4] Meredith D. Clark, "2018 ASNE Newsroom Employment Diversity Survey," New Leaders Association, accessed April 2019, https://members.newsleaders.org/files/Methodology.pdf.

[5] Jenny Gross, "Officer Shot Latino Man Five Times in the Back, Autopsy Says," *The New York Times*, July 10, 2020, https://www.nytimes.com/2020/07/10/us/andres-guardado-police-shooting.html.

[6] "Coroner's Inquest Upholds Earlier Conclusion Andres Guardado's Death Was a Homicide," ABC7 Los Angeles, January 16, 2021, https://abc7.com/andres-guardado-deputy-shooting-inquest-gardena/9707350/; Manthan Chheda, "Andres Guardado: Cops Who Killed Teenage Security Guard Destroyed CCTV Cameras, Seized Video Footage," *International Business Times*, June 20, 2020, https://www.ibtimes.sg/andres-guardado-cops-who-killed-teenage-security-guard-destroyed-cctv-cameras-seized-video-footage-47156.

[7] Julian Samora, Joe Bernal, and Albert Peña, *Gunpowder Justice: A Reassessment of the Texas Rangers* (Notre Dame, IN: University of Notre Dame Press, 1979), 65.

[8] Rebecca Solnit, "Death by gentrification: the killing that shamed San Francisco," *The Guardian,* March 21, 2016, https://www.theguardian.com/us-news/2016/mar/21/death-by-gentrification-the-killing-that-shamed-san-francisco.

[9] "Interview with Diana Palacios," Civil Rights in Black and Brown Oral History Project, Texas Christian University, July 9, 2015, https://crbb.tcu.edu/interviews/100/interview-with-diana-palacios.

[10] Calvin Trillin, "New Cheerleaders," *The New Yorker*, April 17, 1971, https://www.newyorker.com/magazine/1971/04/17/new-cheerleaders.

5. Reclaiming Our Identity

[1] Steven Mintz, "Historical Context: Facts about the Slave Trade and Slavery," the Gilder Lehrman Institute of American History, accessed April 19, 2021, https://www.gilderlehrman.org/history-resources/teaching-resource/historical-context-facts-about-slave-trade-and-slavery.

[2] Nydia Simone, "Latinidad is Cancelled Feat. Alan Pelaez Lopez," SoundCloud, 36:27, accessed April 2021, https://soundcloud.com/nydia-simone/latinidad-is-cancelled-feat-alan-pelaez-lopez.

[3] Ibram X. Kendi, *How to Be an Antiracist* (New York: One World, 2019), 66.

[4] The Root, "Breaking Down the Anti-Blackness of Latinidad," YouTube video, 9:52, September 27, 2019, https://www.youtube.com/watch?v=1Erdq-xhR8M.

[5] Victoria Hattam, *In the Shadow of Race: Jews, Latinos, and Immigrant Politics in the United States* (Chicago: University of Chicago Press, 2007).
[6] David Roediger, *Working Toward Whiteness: How America's Immigrants Became White: The Strange Journey from Ellis Island to the Suburbs* (New York: Basic Books, 2005).

6. Reclaiming Our Culture

[1] Netflix, "Sam Jay Understands Museums Better After Shrooms," YouTube video, 2:24, August 2, 2020, https://www.youtube.com/watch?v=SPjIWPky4ZY.
[2] Russell Contreras, "The Forgotten Anti-Slavery History of Cinco de Mayo," *Axios*, May 5, 2021, https://www.axios.com/cinco-de-mayo-history-anti-slavery-3584ed4d-0e3f-4a75-9fab-02b3bb60fe06.html.
[3] Eduardo Galeano, *Open Veins of Latin America: Five Centuries of the Pillage of a Continent, 25th Anniversary Edition* (New York: Monthly Review Press, 1997), xiii.

7. Last Words

[1] Hector Aguilar, "Los Siete and the Panthers: A Story of Black and Brown solidarity," *El Tecolote*, April 11, 2019, http://eltecolote.org/content/en/los-siete-and-the-panthers-a-story-of-black-and-brown-solidarity/.

About the Author

Julissa Arce is a nationally recognized author, sought-after speaker, producer, and social-change maker. She is the bestselling author of *My (Underground) American Dream* and *Someone Like Me*. Arce is a frequent writer for *Time* magazine and has provided political commentary across numerous TV networks. She is the cofounder of the Ascend Educational Fund, a college scholarship and mentorship program for immigrant students regardless of their immigration status, and she serves on the board of directors of the National Immigration Law Center and Aspire Public Schools. She lives in Los Angeles with her family.